PLAN FOR CRISIS

The World's Leading Emergency Management Manual

Written By

Thomas Anthony Guerriero &
Dr. Lawrence Fenn

TRAFFORD
PUBLISHING™

Order this book online at www.trafford.com
or email orders@trafford.com

Most Trafford titles are also available at major online book retailers.

Printed in the United States of America.

ISBN: 978-1-4669-1403-2 (sc)
ISBN: 978-1-4669-1402-5 (e)

Trafford rev. 02/24/2012

 www.trafford.com

North America & international
toll-free: 1 888 232 4444 (USA & Canada)
phone: 250 383 6864 ♦ fax: 812 355 4082

INTRODUCTION

In today's post September 11th society, it is prevalent now more than ever to have an action plan for any organization to address a plethora of crisis situations. Introducing a detailed plan for crisis management for an organization in dealing with real life situations will increase the probability of survival of an event, while increasing overall safety.

The Plan For Crisis proprietary protocols have been comprised from a wealth of world-class expertise in the planning and management for crisis situations. The authors have expertise in every significant arena related to ensuring the safest and most secure environment possible for all who use this book as a manual to protect their organization. Plan For Crisis offers a wealth of research, leading edge technology, all of which translates to a high-powered comprehensive program to secure the safety of any one who uses it.

ABOUT THE AUTHORS

**Thomas Anthony Guerriero**WMX's founder and Chief Executive Officer (CEO), Mr. Thomas Anthony Guerriero, has over thirteen years of extensive upper executive experience. One of his primary focuses over the course of his career was implementing systems to Plan For Crisis, protecting the organizations greatest assets, the people within the organization. He has led several organizations to be prepared and overcome any crisis situation. This was prevalent in his ability to have a plan in place that allowed for the successful evacuation of his entire organization and their affiliate school from the Financial District on the events of September 11th.

Mr. Guerriero began his career in the financial markets in 1998, and soon thereafter earned the position of Senior Vice President of the securities division of First Union (FTU: NYSE), one of the largest institutions in the world with over $400 billion in client assets. After First Union was acquired by Wachovia, (WB: NYSE) Mr. Guerriero continued to build his client base and team through several institutions and think tanks, eventually etching his name in stone industry wide, by becoming the CEO of a Member Firm, TAA. There he gained the prestigious recognition of being one of the youngest individuals to ever head a member firm.

His success at TAA led him towards the second acquisition in his career, this time by High Point Capital. Mr. Guerriero's unique ability to create unique systems both technical and fundamentally, recruit, train, mentor, and inspire individuals through his creative methodologies has led him to be recognized as a global force to be reckoned with. His most recent acquisition was at the helm of Global Wealth as CEO. He was able to maximize profitability and surpass all expectations, leading towards the third acquisition of his career.

As one of the most talented minds and influential people in the world today he shows no signs in letting up. In 2011, he was nominated, accepted, and confirmed as one of the youngest inductions ever into Marquis's Who's Who in America. Also in 2011 Mr. Guerriero became one of the youngest owners of a professional sports team. He became an owner of a professional basketball team, the Springfield Armor in the NBA D league (The NJ Nets Affiliate). Mr. Guerriero attended Graduate School at Harvard University, holds two Graduate Certificates from Boston University & University of Notre Dame, has two BA degrees from Fairleigh Dickinson University & Thomas Edison State. He has held several licenses over the course of his career Series 7, Series 63, Series 66, Series 24 licenses. He is also a published author with "How To Understand & Master The Stock Market".

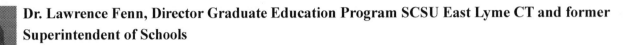 **Dr. Lawrence Fenn, Director Graduate Education Program SCSU East Lyme CT and former Superintendent of Schools**

Dr. Lawrence Fenn is currently President and Owner of Collaborative Education Designs, LLC, where his company develops graduate level programs for Johnson and Wales University and evaluates Federal education programs (Perkins) for Providence and Cranston public schools. Dr. Fenn is also a consultant and advisor to private and public schools in regards to crisis and emergency management.

Prior to owning this company, Dr. Fenn was Superintendent of Schools - Lisbon Public Schools. In this role, Dr. Fenn was responsible for planning, programming, budgeting, monitoring, and managing an educational program for a small progressive school system. As superintendent, Dr. Fenn was instrumental in establishing a partnership with Southern Connecticut State University and the graduate branch of Sacred Heart University. Dr. Fenn has close to 40 years of experience in the field of education and is a member of WMX's advisory board. He has dozens of professional distinctions, honors and awards. He holds a BA and a Master's degree in education.

CONTENTS

EMERGENCIES 2

MEDICAL 3

WEATHER   4

STUDENT WELFARE   5

MEDIA RELATIONS   6

CRISIS TEAM   7

CRISIS TEAM PROCEDURES   8

DISCLAIMER

The information presented in this manual and during any training regarding its use was obtained from sources deemed to be authentic and reliable. No guarantees of results or assumptions of liability in connection with the contents of the manual or presentations by trainers are assumed. Additionally, it should not be assumed that the subject is covered exhaustively or that all procedures outlined would apply to all students. Users of this material are encouraged to adapt or substitute as circumstances, statutes, ordinances, and agency or organizational mandates/policies necessitate.

VIOLENCE/CRIME 1

Weapons/Armed Student

Drive-By Shooting

Out of Control Student

Arguments

Aggressive Acts

Bullying/Intimidation

Trespassers/Loitering

Hostage

Bomb Threat

Bomb Threat Form

Riot/Conflict

Intruders

Sexual Assault/Rape

Sexual Harassment

Stalking

Verbal/Written Suicide Threats

Homicide

Drug Sale

Substance Abuse—Alcohol or Tobacco

Vandalism or Graffiti

WEAPONS/ARMED STUDENT

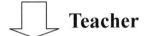 **Teacher**

1.	REMAIN CALM and try to determine if weapon is suspected or visible. **If you see a weapon, RETREAT! DO NOT TRY TO BE A HERO.**
2.	Notify Principal's Office ASAP if possible.
3.	Push Panic Alarms or use Emergency Plan school has in place.
4.	Try to calm student and others while instituting procedures to notify office of event.
5.	**STOP**—DO NOT approach student or attempt to confiscate weapon.
6.	If student is threatening, ask student in a calm voice for permission to evacuate the rest of the class.
7.	Evacuate quickly, if allowed, taking class roll book with you.
8.	Institute plans to ensure teachers keep all students in classrooms until "all clear."
9.	After incident, file reports ASAP.

If Not Allowed to Evacuate: Then:

1.	Keep talking with student until Police arrive.
2.	Ask student to stop what he/she is doing and ask "What is wrong, or what do you want?"
3.	When Police arrive, do as they advise.

Principal's Office

1.	**Call 911 IMMEDIATELY** for Police and security.

If Weapon is Suspected: Then:

1.	Have police bring student to office.
2.	Ensure that at least 2 adults and a Police Officer are present at meeting.
3.	Carefully tell student what is suspected and ask student to produce weapon.
4.	If student agrees, ask student to empty pockets and all other containers.
5.	If search yields nothing, school officials will search student's locker.
6.	If weapon is found, Police Officer will remove student from campus.
7.	Notify parents and Superintendent or designee.
8.	Follow disciplinary action according to code of student conduct.

WEAPONS/ARMED STUDENT (con't)

If Weapon is Visible: **Then:**

1.	**RETREAT! Call 911** immediately.
2.	Notify Superintendent or designee as soon as practical.
3.	Direct Police to scene and work with officers as requested.
4.	Consider announcing request for all students to remain in classrooms if Police authorize you to do so. Use code to lock doors if possible.
5.	Have administrative staff/designee locate and evacuate students who have been locked out of classrooms or are in public areas to safe area outside building.
6.	If advised to do so by Police, evacuate building by PA announcement—**DO NOT** use fire alarm system.
7.	Maintain calm.
8.	Refer media calls to Superintendent.
9.	Notify Crisis Team Media Liaison.
10.	When incident is over, file appropriate reports.

DRIVE-BY SHOOTING

 ## Teacher

1.	If shots are heard, direct students to "drop to the ground" or "drop to the floor."
2.	If car is exiting area, direct students to get inside building quickly.
3.	Be alert for car returning to area.
4.	Be prepared to have students drop to the ground again if necessary.
5.	Notify Principal's office ASAP.
6.	Report any injuries.
7.	Organize students within building and try to restore calm.
8.	Return students to classroom.
9.	Take roll and report any missing students.
10.	Arrange for a classroom monitor.
11.	Return to Principal's office to answer questions from police and/or Administration.

 ## Principal's Office

1.	**Call 911** for police, nurse and ambulance, if necessary.
2.	Notify the Superintendent or designee's office.
3.	Bring all students and staff indoors ASAP.
4.	Secure building by immediately locking doors and windows.
5.	Consider making announcement for teachers in exterior classrooms to order students to drop to the floor.
6.	Have teachers in unaffected areas remain with classes to continue educational process.
7.	Hold students beyond dismissal time if determined to be necessary.
8.	Have staff remain with students until emergency is over.
9.	Advise Superintendent or designee if dismissal will be delayed.
10.	Provide counseling to any students as needed.

OUT of CONTROL STUDENT

 **Teacher**

1.	Notify office to call 911 ASAP!
2.	Send for Counselor, School Psychologist, or social worker.
3.	Evacuate quietly if allowed.
4.	Return students to classroom when advised.
5.	Complete incident reports ASAP!
6.	Identify students who are in need of more intense counseling.

 Principal's Office

1.	**Call 911** for police and ambulance.
2.	Notify nurse to obtain student's emergency health information and take to scene.
3.	Assess if there is a danger to others and take appropriate action.
4.	Turn over scene to Police upon arrival. EMS will be on standby until scene is cleared.
5.	Appoint staff member to handle arriving parents, if any.
6.	Notify Superintendent or designee.
7.	Notify parents.
8.	Notify Crisis Team to convene immediately.

 School Psychologist, Counselor

1.	Personally go to scene and take control.
2.	Determine if event was a suicide or homicide attempt and whether person is in imminent danger i.e., likelihood they would hurt themselves or someone else.
3.	Utilize Beck depression inventory scale and train others in its use in case event takes place when trained personnel not available.
4.	Maintain contact with student during assessment period.
5.	Be careful not to over-react nor under-react.

OUT of CONTROL STUDENT (con't)

 School Psychologist, Counselor (con't)

If Suicide Attempt:　　　　　**Then:**

1.	Take appropriate action if event was a suicide attempt and person is in imminent danger, i.e., if there is likelihood they would hurt themselves or someone else.
2.	Determine in consultation with principal and other staff whether they feel this was a serious attempt and whether commitment criteria for hospitalization have been met.
3.	If criteria have been met, do not allow student to go home with parents due to risk of injury to themselves or others.
4.	If incident is a cry for help that you believe indicates other problems, take appropriate action to facilitate and refer student and parents for treatment.
5.	Proactively ensure that there is a procedure in place, which involves Board of Education and school attorney, for such an event.
6.	Require meeting with you and proof of psychological consultation before student be allowed to return to school.

If Homicidal Attempt:　　　　**Then:**

1.	If event was a homicidal attempt and there is likelihood they would hurt themselves or someone else, take appropriate legal action.
2.	Consult with Police as to their legal standpoint in situation and what they intend to do if they feel a crime has been committed.
3.	Determine in consultation with Principal and other staff whether they feel this was a serious attempt and whether commitment criteria for hospitalization have been met.
4.	If student is being arrested, assist Police. Proactively ensure that there is a procedure in place, which involves Board of Education and school attorney for such an event.
5.	If incident is a cry for help that you believe indicates other problems, take appropriate action to facilitate and refer student and parents for treatment.
6.	Require meeting with you and proof of psychological consultation before student be allowed to return to school.

ARGUMENTS

 **Teacher**   **Principal's Office**

1.	Alert Principal's office of verbal disturbance immediately.
2.	Make verbal contact in calm, low-toned voice.
3.	Ask students to stop; obtain assistance.
4.	If behavior does not cease, shout, "stop" and then lower your voice.
5.	Encourage students to talk about issues someplace else.
6.	Try to get individuals to more isolated area so they can calm themselves.
7.	Try to empty area of other students so there is no audience and less danger to others.
8.	Do not leave student alone until he/ she is calmed down.
9.	Discuss behavior and its consequences only after student is calm.
10.	Do not grab or touch a violent student unless they are likely to cause injury to themselves or others.
11.	If student refuses to cooperate, notify Principal, Special Education Teacher or other appropriate personnel that you need help with a violence problem.

.	Evaluate the severity of the situation ASAP.
2.	When appropriate, call 911 or security.
3.	Activate Crisis Team.
4.	Notify Superintendent or designee's office.
5.	Hold for Administration.

AGGRESSIVE ACTS

Aggressive acts can include: Physical Assaults
                                 Fights
                                 Gang Activity

 ## Teacher

1.	Make verbal contact in calm, low-toned voice.
2.	If behavior does not cease, shout "stop" and then lower your voice.
3.	Ask students to stop; obtain assistance.
4.	Encourage students to talk about issues someplace else.
5.	Try to get individuals to more isolated area so they can calm themselves without losing face.
6.	If preferable, try to empty area of other students so there is not an audience and less danger to others.
7.	Do not leave a student alone until he/she is calmed down.
8.	Discuss behavior and its consequences only after student is calm.
9.	Do not grab or touch a violent student unless they are causing harm to themselves or others.
10.	Give student a choice by clearly stating "You and I must go to the Principal's Office. If you refuse, the police will be called.
11.	If student does refuse to cooperate, notify Principal, Special Education Teacher or other appropriate personnel that you need help with a violence problem.

Principal's Office

1.	Assess situation and intervene if requested by Teacher.
2.	Call security, 911 or parents if students refuse to cooperate.
3.	Notify Superintendent or designee's office.
4.	Hold for administration.
5.	Assist Police in any way requested to facilitate investigation.
6.	Follow disciplinary action according to prescribed code for student conduct.
7.	File an incident report.

BULLYING/INTIMIDATION

<u>Bullying</u> is when physical or verbal coercion in an attempt to control another person or habitual cruelty to others assumed to be weaker is used repeatedly.

<u>Intimidation</u> is the act of attempting to frighten or coerce another person into submitted or obeying.

 **Teacher**

1.	Immediately report to Principal any complaints or personal observation of bullying or intimidation.
2.	File any reports required by school.

Principal's Office

1.	Assess situation and intervene if requested by Teacher.
2.	Notify Superintendent or designee's office.
3.	Follow disciplinary action according to prescribed code for student conduct.
4.	File an incident report.

TRESPASSERS/LOITERING

Trespassers or loiterers are persons who should not be in building but have no apparent intent of malice or violence.

IF TRESPASSER or
LOITERER INBUILDING: **Then:**

1.	Notify main office there is a trespasser or loitering in the building if person does not have ominous intent.
2.	Call 911 with description and if known, give: Name Intent Location in Building
3.	Take action for precautions to be taken i.e. use code to have classroom teachers take precautions until status is known.
4.	ALL CLASSROOM STAFF WILL: • Close and lock doors • Close windows • Await further instructions.
5.	Administrative team will be notified.
6.	Office will announce "All Clear" when situation is resolved.

HOSTAGE

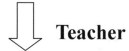 **Teacher**

1.	Notify Principal's office ASAP and advise if weapon is suspected/visible.
2.	Trigger panic alarm or other alarm system provided to alert office and Police that incident is in progress.
3.	Try to calm student being held and perpetrator or others in area while instituting procedure to notify office of event. Push Panic Alarm or use Emergency Plan school has in place.
4.	**STOP-DO NOT approach student** or attempt to confiscate weapon.
5.	If weapon is visible or student is threatening to injure person being held, ask student in a calm voice for permission to evacuate the rest of the class.
6.	Evacuate quietly, if allowed, taking class roll book with you.
7.	Institute Crisis and Emergency Management plan to ensure teachers hold all students in rooms until "all clear."

If Not Allowed to Evacuate: Then:

1.	Keep talking with student until Police arrive.
2.	Ask student to stop what he/she is doing and ask "What is wrong, or what do you want?" NOTE: Proper language is important and prior training is advisable.
3.	Tell students in area to protect themselves with desks, equipment, or tables.
4.	Try to maintain communication with perpetrator in calm manner.
5.	When Police arrive, do as they direct if they are allowed to communicate.
6.	After incident, file reports ASAP.

HOSTAGE (con't)

 Principal's Office

1.	**Call 911 IMMEDIATELY** for Police and security.

If Weapon is Suspected: **Then:**

1.	Have Police bring student to office.
2.	Ensure that at least 2 adults and a Police Office are present at meeting.
3.	Carefully tell student what is suspected and ask student to produce weapon.
4.	Ask student to empty pockets and all other containers.
5.	If search yields nothing, school officials will search student's locker.
6.	If weapon is found, Police Officer will remove student from campus.
7.	Notify parents and Superintendent or designee.
8.	Follow disciplinary action according to code of student conduct.

If Weapon is Visible: **Then:**

1.	Notify Superintendent's office.
2.	Turn over control of situation to Police upon their arrival.
3.	If advised by Police, consider announcing request for all students to remain in classrooms. **Note: Use code to lock doors if possible.**
4.	Have administrative staff/designee evacuate students who have been locked out of classrooms or are in public areas to pre-arranged safe area outside building.
5.	If advised to do so by police, evacuate building by PA announcement—**DO NOT** use fire alarm system.
6.	Maintain calm.
7.	Refer media calls to Superintendent.
8.	Notify Crisis Team Media Liaison.

BOMB THREAT

1.	Maintain calm while collecting class roster.
2.	Evacuate if advised.
3.	**If evacuation is necessary, instruction will be relayed to classrooms.**
4.	Open windows and follow pre-arranged evacuation route or route indicated in announcement.
5.	Take attendance when students are assembled away from school building.
6.	Advise administration and counselors if student is missing.

⬇ Recipient of Bomb Threat by Telephone

⬇ Principal's Office

1.	Keep caller on the telephone as long as possible—do NOT hang up. NOTE: If student answers phones, get adult to phone if possible.
2.	Use **Bomb Threat Checklist** that should be kept within reach, to prompt you as to what to ask. Document your observations. NOTE: These blank forms should be easily within reach of clerical staff and others who answer telephones. Keeping a laminated copy on a hook near office telephones is recommended.
3.	Utilize telephone options of caller I.D., *57, and *69 which will allow telephone company to track and track call.
4.	Brief police and school administration as to specifics and observations.
5.	File incident report.

1.	Call 911 **IMMEDIATELY** and evacuate building.
2.	Notify Superintendent or designee's office.
3.	Do not use radios or electric bells as they can activate bombs.
4.	Pass information and instructions to teachers via selected personnel.
5.	**DO NOT TOUCH** any suspicious packages.
6.	Remain in office to coordinate search and work with police.
7.	Notify Crisis Team Media Liaison.
8.	File incident report.
9.	Refer media to Superintendent.
10.	Establish a Unified Incident Command Post.

 **Teacher**

BOMB THREAT CHECKLIST

CALLER'S VOICE:

_____ Calm	_____ Angry	_____ Excited	_____ Slow
_____ Rapid	_____ Soft	_____ Loud	_____ Laughter
_____ Crying	_____ Normal	_____ Distinct	_____ Slurred
_____ Nasal	_____ Stutter	_____ Lisp	_____ Raspy
_____ Deep	_____ Ragged	_____ Clearing Throat	_____ Deep Breathing
_____ Accent	_____ Familiar	_____ Cracking Voice	_____ Disguised

If voice is familiar who did it sound like? _____

BACKGROUND SOUNDS:

_____ Crockery	_____ Voices	_____ Street Noises	_____ PA System
_____ Music	_____ Motor	_____ Office Machinery	_____ House Noises
_____ Clear	_____ Static	_____ Factory Machinery	_____ Animal noises
_____ Local	_____ Booth	_____ Long Distance	

Other: _____

THREAT LANGUAGE:

_____ Foul	_____ Irrational	_____ Well Spoken	_____ Incoherent
_____ Tapes	_____ Message read by threat maker		

REMARKS:_____

QUESTIONS TO ASK:

1. When is the bomb going to explode?
_____

2. Where is it right now?
_____

3. What does it look like?
_____

4. What kind of bomb is it?
_____

5. What will cause it to explode?
_____

6. Did you place the bomb?
_____

7. Why?
_____

8. What is your address?
_____

9. What is your name?
_____

Exact wording of threat:

_____

Sex of caller: ___ Race: ___ Age: ___ Length of Call: ___ Time: ___ Date: ____ Number of call received:

Date: _____ Name: _____ Phone number: _____ Position: _____

NOTE: It is recommended that this checklist be laminated and kept near telephones and within reach of those who usually answer calls. It can then be easily seen and used as a guide as to what to do should a bomb threat call occur.

RIOT or CONFLICT

 **Teacher**

1.	Alert Principal's office immediately if problem occurs.
2.	Make verbal contact with involved students in calm, low-toned voice.
3.	Ask students to stop; obtain assistance.
4.	If behavior does not cease, shout, "stop" and then lower your voice.
5.	Encourage students to talk about issues someplace else.
6.	Try to get individuals to more isolated area so they can calm themselves.
7.	If preferable, try to empty area of other students so there is not an audience and less danger to others.
8.	Do not leave student alone until he/she is calmed down.
9.	Discuss behavior and its consequences only after student is calm.
10.	Do not grab or touch a violent student unless they are in imminent danger of causing harm to themselves or others.
11.	If student does refuse to cooperate, notify Principal, Special Education Teacher or other appropriate personnel that you need help with a violence problem.

 Principal's Office

1.	Evaluate the severity of the situation ASAP.
2.	When appropriate, call 911 or security.
3.	Activate administrative support team.

RIOT or CONFLICT (con't)

 **Principal's Office**

Be Prepared to:

1.	Bring all students and staff indoors.
2.	Lock all windows and doors.
3.	Deny unauthorized access to building.
4.	Advise students and staff of situation.
5.	Hold students beyond dismissal time when necessary.

If Conflict is in Building:  Then

1.	Speak in calm, low-toned voice.
2.	If behavior does not cease, shout "stop" then lower voice.
3.	Encourage students to talk about issues someplace else.
4.	Never grab or touch violent students unless they are causing harm to themselves or others.
5.	Continue calm-voice, reasonable-force approaches until opposition factions are separated and/or police arrive.
6.	Cooperate with police.
7.	Identify participating students and any gang affiliations.
8.	Discuss the students' behavior and its consequences only after they are calm.
9.	Notify parents or those listed on emergency release form.
10.	File an incident report form.

INTRUDERS

Intruders are persons on the premises with intents of malice, mischief, violence, and/or destruction.

 **Teacher**

1.	Report any suspicious person to Principal's office immediately.
2.	If person threatening ask office to call 911.
3.	Institute procedure for "Lock Down" via announcement over intercom using secret code to lock doors.
4.	In classroom: • Close and lock doors • Close windows • Keep children quiet and in room until "all clear" is sounded • Those closest to bathrooms should quickly check for children. Keep any students found in your room until "all clear" is given • Await further instructions.

Principal's Office

1.	Ensure **911** is called immediately!
2.	Approach the intruders and determine the nature of their presence. Ask for identification.
3.	Direct and/or accompany them to proper office.
4.	Ask individual(s) to leave if they have no acceptable purpose and escort them personally to nearest exit.
5.	Remind individuals they are in violation of the law if they refuse to leave.
6.	Alert individuals that police will be called.
7.	Call 911 to police if they still refuse to leave.
8.	Initiate LOCK DOWN PROCEDURES.
9.	Have administrative staff evacuate any students locked out of classrooms to pre-planned safe location.
10.	Establish a Unified Incident Command Post.
11.	Notify Superintendent or designee.
12.	File an incident report.

INTRUDERS

"LOCK-DOWN" PROCEDURE

When warranted, the main office will initiate a **"LOCK-DOWN" PROCEDURE**. The following protocol must be put into place immediately when announcement is made:

 **Teacher**

1.	Lock all doors. Close all windows. Call office for missing students.
2.	Keep students quiet and in room. No one is to leave room under any circumstance.
3.	Classes closest to bathroom will check and remove student to room. Call office to notify.
4.	Call office for emergency.
5.	Await further instruction.
6.	Upon hearing "clear" signal resume regular schedule.

 **Principal's Office**

1.	Announce **"All students and staff initiate lockdown procedure."**
2.	Notify all classes outside of building to report to the Senior Center.
3.	Contact custodians. Lock and check all outer doors.
4.	When "clear" announce, "All clear, Mr. Lock has left the building."

\

SEXUAL ASSAULT/RAPE

 **Teacher**

1.	Notify Principal's office immediately.
2.	Complete incident report, noting need for confidentiality.

 **Principal's Office**

1.	Call parents and notify Police of incident to protect criminal case should one result.
2.	Call Nurse to pull emergency health information from enrollment card and to administer first aid to victim.
3.	Call grade level School Psychologist or Counselor to stay with victim.
4.	Isolate suspect, if possible.
5.	Isolate witnesses and do not allow them to talk to anyone or to each other, respecting confidentiality.
6.	Convene crisis team.
7.	Notify Superintendent or designee.
8.	Facilitate any investigations by district and civil authorities.
9.	Review and complete incident report.

 **Drivers, Cafeteria Staff, Playground Aides, Student Interns**

1.	Notify Principal's office immediately should you suspect or observe any type of sexual or inappropriate assault.
2.	Complete incident report, which are to be kept confidential. Any adult with responsibility for or access to students must report suspected incidents.

SEXUAL HARASSMENT

Sexual Harassment is unwelcome conduct, verbal or physical, of a sexual nature. This could include insulting/ degrading sexual conduct or remarks; suggestions that submitting to or rejecting unwelcome advances would influence a decision about a student or staff member; or conduct which would interfere with student learning, creating intimidating, hostile, offensive learning/working environment i.e. display of sexually suggestive object/pictures.

Teacher

1.	Alert Principal's office immediately.
2.	Complete incident report, noting need for confidentiality.

Principal's Office

1.	Call parents and notify Police of incident to protect criminal case should one result.
2.	Call Nurse to pull emergency health information from enrollment card and to administer counseling to victim.
3.	Call grade level School Psychologist or counselor to stay with victim.
4.	Isolate suspect, if possible.
5.	Isolate witnesses and do not allow them to talk to anyone or to each other, respecting confidentiality.
6.	Notify parents to come to school.
7.	Notify Superintendent or designee.
8.	Facilitate any investigations by district and civil authorities.
9.	Review and complete incident report.

Bus Drivers, Cafeteria Staff, Playground Aides, Student Interns

1.	Alert Principal's office immediately should you suspect or observe any type of sexual or inappropriate assault.
2.	Complete incident report, noting need for confidentiality. Any adult with responsibility for or access to students must report suspected incidents.

STALKING

 **Teacher**

1.	Alert Principal's office immediately if a student reports a stalking incident to you.
2.	Complete incident report, noting need for confidentiality.
3.	Ensure diary of stalking activities is kept.

 **Principal's Office**

1.	Call parents and notify Police of suspected stalking to protect criminal case should one result.
2.	Call grade level School Psychologist or Counselor to speak with victim.
3.	If a student, isolate suspected stalker.
4.	Document date(s) of incident of stalking.
5.	Review and complete incident report.

 Bus Drivers, Cafeteria Staff, Playground Aides, Student Interns

1.	Alert Principal's office immediately should you suspect or observe any type of stalking activity or if a student reports they are being stalked.
2.	Complete incident report, noting need for confidentiality. Any adult with responsibility for or access to students must report suspected incidents.

VERBAL/WRITTEN SUICIDE THREATS

 **Teacher**

 **School Psychologist, Counselor**

1.	Notify school counselor immediately.
2.	Take threats seriously; keep student stable.
3.	Tell student you are concerned.
4.	Do not leave student alone.
5.	Continue to monitor and express interest in student after crisis is over.

1.	Isolate student from peers if possible and initiate protocol to assess seriousness of threat.
2.	Talk with student and assess their state of mind.
3.	Ask directly if person has entertained thoughts of suicide or if they feel depressed.
4.	**Do not** leave student alone.
5.	Notify Principal and parents.
6.	Continue to counsel and observe the student, documenting observations until situation is calm.
7.	If incident is a cry for help that you believe indicates other problems, take appropriate action to facilitate and refer student and parents for treatment.
8.	Determine in consultation with Principal and other staff whether they fell this was a serious attempt and whether commitment criteria for hospitalization have been met.
9.	Provide student and parents with other community resources for counseling should they be allowed to return home.
10.	Require meeting with you and/or Principal and proof of psychological consultation before student be allowed to return to school.
11.	Work with parents, student, administrators and teacher to monitor and reassess student periodically.

VERBAL/WRITTEN SUICIDE THREATS (con't)

 **Principal's Office**

1.	In absence of School Psychologist, take control of situation and isolate student from peers if possible.
2.	Talk with student and assess the seriousness of threat.
3.	Ask directly if person has entertained thoughts of suicide or if they feel depressed.
4.	**Do not** leave student alone.
5.	Notify parents to come to school immediately.
6.	If incident is a cry for help that you and other staff believe indicates other problems, take appropriate action to facilitate and refer student and parents for treatment.
7.	Documents observations and actions, particularly in absence of trained psychologist.
8.	Complete required form for Superintendent/designee.
9.	In postvention period, send letter to parents referring to school policy for these types of occurrences.
10.	Require meeting with you and/or School Psychologist or Counselor and proof of psychological consultation before student be allowed to return to school.

If Suicide was Prevented: Then:

1.	Authorize increased counseling services to students/staff that were involved in incident.
2.	Be certain parents are required to show proof of psychological consultation for student and themselves before student is allowed to return to school.

If Suicide was Not Prevented: Then:

1.	Authorize increased counseling services to students and staff.
2.	Provide written and personal condolences to family.
3.	Facilitate any investigations by district/civil authorities.
4.	Convene Crisis Team to analyze how incident was handled and make changes to any procedures or policies if necessary.

HOMICIDE

 **Teacher**

1.	Notify office to call 911. Office will notify Principal's Office and the nurse.
2.	If perpetrator is in the area, speak calmly until police arrive and rely on confrontation training procedures as to what to say.
3.	If a weapon is involved, **RETREAT IMMEDIATELY** and evacuate as much of immediate area as is safe.
4.	If there is no perpetrator, remove students from the area.
5.	Await police arrival and secure scene. **Do not disturb anything in area, as this is a crime scene!**
6.	Separate any witnesses to incident.
7.	Identify students or teachers in need of treatment for shock.
8.	Complete incident reports ASAP.

Principal's Office

1.	Ensure 911 are called for police and ambulance. Notify them if a weapon is visible and if so what type i.e., gun, knife, other.
2.	Ensure emergency health information is obtained from enrollment card.
3.	Await police arrival, brief them as to what type of weapon is involved, if any. Turn over scene to them immediately.
4.	Notify Superintendent or designee.
5.	Convene school crisis team to handle logistics of postvention activities.
6.	Inform staff and inform students in an appropriate manner with crisis team.
7.	Facilitate investigations by civil authorities i.e., police, DCF.
8.	Organize counseling services and document students/staff in need of treatment for shock or counseling.
9.	Write informational note to parents including condolences.
10.	File an incident report.

 **Nurse**

1.	Check vital signs to determine if death has occurred while providing privacy for victim.
2.	Document approximate time and specific observations.
3.	Secure emergency health information from enrollment card.
4.	Provide copy of documented information to EMS for hospital personnel.
5.	File incident report.

DRUG SALE (SUSPECTED)

 **Teacher**

 **Nurse**

1.	Notify office on witnessing a possible drug sale, usage or possession.
2.	Call 911 to notify State Police and while waiting for their arrival: Do not destroy or touch evidence Keep student involved and isolated until authorities arrive If drug use is admitted to or otherwise verified, EMS will respond for transportation to Emergency Room Keep any witnesses separated
3.	If drug abuse is suspected, refer matter to administration for evaluation.
4.	If evidence is obtained, turn student and substance over to Principal or designee.
5.	Complete incident reports ASAP.

1.	Conduct an emergency assessment.
2.	Administer first aid until medical personnel arrive. If person is obviously under the influence of some substance, try to keep them calm and stable.
3.	Appoint staff member to secure emergency information, accompany student to hospital, and act as liaison.
4.	Document findings.
5.	If student is alert, obtain name or drug, how administered and at what time.
6.	Provide copy of document information to EMS for hospital personnel.
7.	File an incident report.

DRUG SALE (SUSPECTED) (con't)

 **Principal's Office**

1.	Ensure 911 has been called and if student is ill, refer to nurse ASAP.
2.	Assist nurse in making assessment.
3.	Maintain integrity of any evidence while waiting for State Police to arrive. DO NO TOUCH any suspicious substances since some can be absorbed through the skin!
4.	Have police officer bring student to office with possessions, ensuring that at least 2 adults and police officer are present.
5.	Tell student what is suspected and ask student to produce drugs.
6.	If student denies or refuses, ask student to empty pockets and all containers.

**If Drug is Found
or Sale is Witnessed:**   **Then:**

1.	Police officer will remove student from campus.
2.	Notify parent or those listed on emergency release form.
3.	Contact the Superintendent or designee.
4.	Follow disciplinary action according to school and Board policies.
5.	Suggest student enroll in drug counseling program.

If No Drug is Found: **Then:**

1.	Call for nurse to make impairment assessment.
2.	Notify a parent to come to school.
3.	Meet with student, parent and a counselor.
4.	Follow disciplinary action according to school and Board of Education policies.

SUBSTANCE ABUSE with ALCOHOL or TOBACCO

 **Teacher**

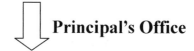 **Principal's Office**

1.	Notify Principal's office or designee or suspected use or possession of alcohol or tobacco.
2.	If drug abuse is suspected, refer matter to administration for evaluation.
3.	If evidence is obtained, turn student and substance over to Principal or designee.
4.	Complete incident reports ASAP.

1.	Bring student to office with backpack, purse, books and/or other possessions.
2.	Two additional adults should be present.
3.	Tell student what is suspected and ask them to produce alcohol or tobacco.
4.	Question student regarding involvement of others.
5.	If student denies usage, ask him/her to empty pockets and containers and search locker if needed.
6.	If alcohol or tobacco is found or if usage is witnessed, notify parents.
7.	Contact Superintendent or designee's office.
8.	Follow disciplinary action according to school and Board policies.
9.	File an incident report.

VANDALISM or GRAFFITI

 **Teacher**

1.	Notify Principal's Office of damage and names of vandals, if known.

Principal's Office

1.	Assess extent of damage; if major, contact Superintendent or designee.
2.	Be certain photos of graffiti are taken immediately since each "artist" has their own look and photos are kept on file in police departments for ID purposes.
3.	Contact insurance carrier and report vandalism.

If Damage is Minor: **Then**

1.	Direct custodian to assess, clean and/or repair.
2.	If additional help required, custodian is to contact maintenance office.

If Damage is Major: **Then**

1.	Cordon off area as appropriate.
2.	Call 911 if necessary.
3.	Notify Superintendent or designee or maintenance office.
4.	Take photos of damage with cameras kept in office.
5.	Make notes on kind, extent, location and approximate time of incurred damage.
6.	Attempt to identify vandals.
7.	Identify witnesses.
8.	File appropriate criminal charges against vandals.

If Student is Identified: **Then**

1.	Notify parents or those listed on emergency release form.
2.	Follow disciplinary action.
3.	File complete report of damage or loss of property with Superintendent or designee.
4.	After police have seen damage, call custodial services for clean up.

EMERGENCIES 2

Bus Accident
Fire or Explosion
Gas Leak
Power Outage
Power Line Down
Building Operability Checklist
Evacuation
Shelter in Building
Hazardous Material Release
Incompatible Materials Chart
Asbestos Release
Bio-Chemical Terrorism
Water Shortage

BUS ACCIDENT

 **Bus Driver**

1.	Administer first aid to any critically injured students then call 911 for Police and EMS.
2.	Secure vehicle and display appropriate warning devices.
3.	Survey all individuals involved in the accident for extent of injuries, remaining calm.
4.	Call Supervisor.
5.	Report the location of accident, bus number and route number.
6.	Report any injuries and whether an ambulance is needed.
7.	Report whether a bus is needed to continue route.
8.	Keep all students on bus unless safety conditions warrant removal.
9.	Recruit adult assistance by flagging approaching vehicles, if absolutely necessary.
10.	DO NOT move vehicle until instructed to do so.
11.	Get list of students on that particular bus, account for all students and on proper form and record extent of injuries.
12.	Get names, addresses and phone numbers of all witnesses and respond to telephone calls from parents and media.
13.	Make no statements to media or bystanders; give information to investigating officers and school officials only.
14.	Upon returning to transportation department, assist in completing all necessary accident reports.

If Threat of Fire: **Then:**

1.	Move children and others to safe location, at least 100' from side of road if possible.

BUS ACCIDENT (con't)

Principal's Office

1.	Notify Superintendent's Office to ensure necessary Administrators are notified.
2.	Collect emergency health information from enrollment cards for all students on bus.
3.	Appoint 2-3 staff members with visible ID's to go to accident site to bring any special health considerations to medical personnel at site.
4.	If an ambulance has been called, a staff member should accompany ambulance to the hospital with emergency health information and act as liaison between hospital and school.
5.	In the event of a serious injury or fatality, the Principal/designee will go to accident site and hospital.
6.	Appoint staff to contact parents and, as information is available, inform them whether their child is injured or uninjured or to direct them to medical facility to which student has been taken. Connect-ED activated.
7.	Assemble Crisis Team.
8.	Refer incoming media calls to Superintendent's office or to Crisis Team Media Relations.

District Bus Coordinator

1.	Go to scene of accident ASAP bringing guidelines, forms, and camera and radio or cell phone.
2.	If medical personnel have not arrived, assist with first aid.
3.	Get list of students involved in accident, type of injuries incurred and, report new information to central dispatch if possible.
4.	Take pictures of accident scene, gather information, and compile seating chart at time of accident.
5.	Assist bus driver in any way possible, including caring for students.
6.	Go to the hospital and stay until a physician has seen everyone.
7.	Refer media to Superintendent or Media Liaison.
8.	Complete accident report and forward to district safety department, transportation office, and/or other designated officials.

BUS ACCIDENT (con't)

Use diagram to indicate where each student who was on bus was sitting at time of accident.

Front of Bus

Bus No. _____

Time of Incident: _____ AM ____ PM____

Driver Name:

Date of Incident: _____

<u>Seating</u>

_____	1	_____
_____	2	_____
_____	3	_____
_____	4	_____
_____	5	_____
_____	6	_____
_____	7	_____
_____	8	_____
_____	9	_____
_____	10	_____
_____	11	_____

FIRE or EXPLOSION

 **Principal's Office**

 **Teacher**

	Principal's Office
1.	Use PA announcement if alternative route or area is to be used.
2.	Sound alarm to signal evacuation to pre-designated route.
3.	Ensure Custodian and cafeteria staff has turned off all power equipment.
4.	Activate procedure for parent notification.
5.	Ensure appointed caretakers assist handicapped students.
6.	Call 911 if alarm does not sound.
7.	Advise nurse and staff to administer first aid as needed and call ambulance if needed.
8.	Evacuate all staff to pre-designated routes.
9.	Notify Superintendent's Office.
10.	After total roster is collected, have pre-appointed staff search for missing students.
11.	Notify area emergency services director of missing students, if any.

	Teacher
1.	Evacuate when alarm sounds.
2.	Check accuracy of pre-designated evacuation routes posted inside each classroom door, take roster and grade book.
3.	Close classroom door and leave lights as they are.
4.	Leave building in orderly manner without rushing or crowding.
5.	Reassemble students in safe area.
6.	Report missing students immediately.
7.	Note on roster students released to parents.
8.	Return to room when instructed to do so.

FIRE or EXPLOSION (con't)

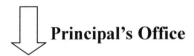 **Principal's Office**

1.	Use PA announcement if alternative route or area is to be used.
2.	Sound alarm to signal evacuation to pre-designated route.
3.	Ensure Custodian and cafeteria staff has turned off all power equipment.
4.	Activate procedure for parent notification.
5.	Ensure appointed caretakers assist handicapped students.
6.	Call 911 if alarm does not sound.
7.	Advise nurse and staff to administer first aid as needed and call ambulance if needed.
8.	Evacuate all staff to pre-designated routes.
9.	Notify Superintendent's Office.
10.	After total roster is collected, have pre-appointed staff search for missing students.
11.	Notify town emergency services director of missing students.

If Evacuating to other Site: **Then:**

1.	Organize bus-loading system.

If Students are Dismissed: **Then:**

1.	Establish a checkout area.
2.	Release students only to parents or those listed on emergency forms.
3.	Signal "All Clear—Return to Class" when appropriate.
4.	File an incident report.

GAS LEAK

 **Teacher**

1.	Evacuate students to assembly point when informed to do so.
2.	Use fire drill procedures for evacuation.
3.	**STOP! Do Not Operate Electrical Switches**
4.	Route students around and away from areas of strong gas odor.
5.	Take roll call at assembly point.
6.	Ensure that medical care is given to anyone injured or overcome by gas.
7.	Relocate students to Designated assembly point as soon as feasible.

 **Principal's Office**

1.	Notify building occupants by bullhorn or oral announcement to evacuate whenever a strong gas odor is reported.
2.	**STOP! DO NOT USE** fire alarm signal as it may take students into areas of highest gas concentration.
3.	Call 911 and report smell of gas.
4.	Notify gas company.
5.	Notify Superintendent's office to ensure that necessary administrators are notified.
6.	Oversee evacuation to designated assembly point.
7.	In conjunction with authorities, determine when building is safe for re-occupancy.
8.	File an incident report.

Custodian

1.	Ventilate area, starting where gas concentration is strongest.
2.	Operate manual controls to shut off open flame devices.
3.	**STOP! DO NOT OPERATE Electrical Switches!**
4.	Notify gas company and assist gas company personnel in finding and fixing gas leak.
5.	Use "Building Operability Checklist"—CEM to determine if building can be occupied.
6.	Advise Principal when building is safe for re-occupancy.

POWER OUTAGE

 **Cafeteria Staff**

1.	Prepare cold food menus when possible.
2.	Monitor food storage temperatures.
3.	Notify Food Services Director.

Teacher

1.	Follow instructions from Principal's office.
2.	Keep children calm while waiting for power to come back on.

Custodian

1.	Distribute available flashlights.
2.	Activate emergency generator or lighting if available.
3.	Assist power company if requested.

Teacher

1.	Instruct occupants of building to either remain in place or evacuate by using bullhorn or messenger.
2.	Inform power company of outage.
3.	Notify Superintendent's office.
4.	Notify cafeteria to take appropriate action.

POWER LINE DOWN

 **Custodian**

1.	Distribute available flashlights.
2.	Activate emergency generator or lighting if available.
3.	Assist power company if requested.

 **Principal's Office**

1.	Call 911 immediately for Police and Fire Department assistance.
2.	Instruct occupants of building to either remain in place or evacuate by using bullhorn or messenger.
3.	Notify building occupants by bullhorn or messenger if PA system has failed.
4.	Activate procedure for parent notification.
5.	Be certain power company designated liaison guards area where downed power line is located.
6.	Inform power company of outage.
7.	Notify Superintendent's office.
8.	File incident report.

 **Teacher**

1.	Report power line location if visible to you.
2.	Keep children away from windows.

BUILDING OPERABILITY CHECKLIST

This checklist is to be used when assessing a building's ability to be operational following a major storm such as a hurricane or after any type of emergency where building is affected.

ITEM	OPERATIONAL	DAMAGED
Water availability Water Contamination	☐Y ☐N ☐Y ☐N	☐Y ☐N ☐Y ☐N
Gas availability Gas Leakage/Smell	☐Y ☐N ☐Y ☐N	☐Y ☐N ☐Y ☐N
Electricity availability	☐Y ☐N	☐Y ☐N
Sanitation system functioning	☐Y ☐N	☐Y ☐N
HVAC functioning	☐Y ☐N	☐Y ☐N
Boilers functioning	☐Y ☐N	☐Y ☐N
Roof leaks	☐Y ☐N	☐Y ☐N
Fallen trees	☐Y ☐N	☐Y ☐N
Fallen electrical wires **DO NOT TOUCH!**	☐Y ☐N	☐Y ☐N
Windows, doors damaged	☐Y ☐N	☐Y ☐N
Water lines, plumbing damaged	☐Y ☐N	☐Y ☐N
Flooding	☐Y ☐N	☐Y ☐N
Hazardous Materials contained?	☐Y ☐N	☐Y ☐N
Misc.	☐Y ☐N	☐Y ☐N

EVACUATION

Emergencies requiring evacuation include:

Drills	Disasters	Fire
Fallen Aircraft	Chemical Release	Bomb Threat

 **School Nurse**

1.	Administer first aid if necessary.
2.	Assist emergency medical personnel as requested.
3.	File necessary reports.
4.	Close classroom door and turn out lights as students leave.

Teacher

1.	Evacuate if you hear signal for evacuation or call on PA system.
2.	Be aware of pre-designated primary and alternate evacuation routes.
3.	Take roster sheet and grade book with you.
4.	Close classroom door and turn out lights as students leave.
5.	Leave building in orderly manner without rushing.
6.	If situation warrants, vehicle will be used to transport students to another site.
7.	For evacuation without vehicles, walk from building in stated course.
8.	Always evacuate cross wind and/or upwind.
9.	Evacuate students to at least 300 feet from building and out of way of emergency vehicles.
10.	Reassemble students and check roll to account for all students.
11.	Report any missing students immediately.
12.	Note on roster students released to parents.
13.	If students are to be evacuated to another site or dismissed, organize system for loading buses.
14.	Return to classroom when instructed to do so.

EVACUATION (con't)

 **Principal's Office**

1.	Sound signal for evacuation. Use PA announcement if alternate evacuation route or assembly area is to be used.
2.	Call 911 for Police and/or fire department.
3.	Advise whether ambulances are needed.
4.	Advise Nurse and staff to administer first aid if necessary.
5.	Evacuate all staff and students using pre-designated evacuation routes.
6.	Ensure that caretakers assist handicapped students.
7.	Ensure pre-appointed staff should search building for stragglers.
8.	Ensure that custodian and cafeteria staff has turned off all power equipment.
9.	Notify Superintendent or designee's office to ensure that necessary Administrators are notified.
10.	Advise whether primary or alternate assembly area will be used.
11.	Advise whether students need to be transported by bus to another site.
12.	Establish a Unified Incident Command Post.
13.	After total roster is collected, pre-appointed staff members search building for any missing students.
14.	If students are to be evacuated to another site or dismissed, organize system for loading buses.
15.	If students are to be dismissed, establish checkout area.
16.	Students should be release ONLY to parents or those listed on emergency release form.
17.	Signal "All Clear—return to class" when appropriate.
18.	File an incident report.

USE of SHELTER in BUILDING

A decision to "Shelter in Building" or evacuate must be made.

 **Teacher**

1.	Move all students indoors.
2.	Close all windows and doors to the shelter.
3.	Turn off room heating, cooling or ventilation systems.
4.	If suspected air contamination within shelter, place wet handkerchief or wet paper towels over nose and mouth for temporary respiratory protection and instruct children to do the same.
5.	Continue to follow the instructions given over the PA system.
6.	Do not allow anyone to leave shelter until the "all clear" is given.

DEFINITION:

Shelter in Building is the use of any Classroom or office for the purpose of providing temporary shelter from a hazardous material release.

POSSIBLE EMERGENCY:

Hazardous Material Release
- Chemical Plant Accident
- Chemical Train Derailment
- Chemical Truck Overturning
- Pipeline Rupture
- Bio-Chemical Terrorism
Drill

Principal's Office

1.	Make decision based on information or instructions to shelter in place, due to nearby hazardous material releases or other emergency procedure.
2.	Activate school "shelter in place" announce over PA system, and activate procedure for parent notification.
3.	Instruct all persons in outside areas to go indoors.
4.	Ensure that appointed caretakers assist handicapped students and designate individual to do a building sweep when everyone is thought to be evacuated.
5.	Ensure maintenance immediately shuts off all heating, cooling and ventilation systems for entire campus.
6.	Consider instructing teachers to seal doors and windows with duct tape in severe cases.
7.	Notify the Superintendent or designee's office.
8.	DO NOT allow anyone to leave shelter during the emergency.
9.	Use reasonable judgment in allowing outsiders into shelter during height of incident.
10.	Keep in contact with police and Superintendent's office for continuous information and instructions until incident is under control.
11.	Announce current status of incident at frequent intervals over PA system until "all clear."

HAZARDOUS MATERIAL RELEASE

 **Principal's Office**

1.	Call 911 immediately for State Police and EMS.
2.	Activate procedure for parent notification.
3.	Consult with Fire department officials as to whether to "Shelter in Building" or evacuate.

If Told to Shelter: **Then:**

1.	Follow "Shelter in Place" procedure.

If Told to Evacuate: **Then:**

1.	Follow evacuation procedures.

HAZARDOUS MATERIAL EMERGENCIES:
- Chemical Plant Accident
- Chemical Train Derailment
- Chemical Truck Overturning
- Pipeline Rupture
- Outside Gas Leak
- Bio-Chemical Terrorism
- Other Bio-Chemical Contaminants

ASBESTOS RELEASE

Principal's Office

	GENERAL INFORMATION

1. Asbestos is not considered hazardous unless it is airborne as dust fibers.
2. Most asbestos-containing building Materials are products such as floor tiles, window putty, pipe insulation and ceiling tiles. These will not release airborne asbestos fibers unless they are significantly disturbed.
3. Under the Federal Asbestos Hazardous Emergency Response Act (AHERA), all schools should be re-inspected every six months to re-evaluate conditions.

1.	Evacuate building if asbestos has been released.
2.	Notify Superintendent or designee's office.
3.	Close doors and isolate affected area as much as possible.
4.	Notify custodian to shut down heating, ventilation and air conditioning units.
5.	Notify Superintendent or designee's office.
6.	Report incident to area health department.
7.	Assist district and local officials as needed.
8.	File incident report to include names of students in the area.

Noxious Chemical/Materials Interaction

| MATERIAL GROUP | EXAMPLE | INCOMPATIBLE MATERIALS | EXAMPLES | REACTION IF MIXED |

1. This Chart is to be used as **GUIDE ONLY!**
2. For <u>specific information</u> on storage of Hazardous Materials, consult the Material Supply Data Sheet ("MSDS") log.

ASBESTOS RELEASE

MATERIAL GROUP	EXAMPLE	INCOMPATIBLE MATERIALS	EXAMPLES	REACTION IF MIXED
ACIDS	Battery-Acid Paint Removers De-Rust Sprays	FLAMMABLES/COMBUSTIGLES ALKALIES/CAUSTICS/BASES OXIDIZERS	Degreasers, Carbon Removers, Antifogging Compounds	HEAT VIOLENT GAS GENERATION REACTION
ADHESIVES	Epoxies Isocyanates Diethylenetri amine	ACIDS ALKALIES/CAUSTICS/BASES OXIDIZERS		HEAT FIRE HAZARD
ALKALIES BASES/ CAUSTICS	Ammonia Sodium Hydroxide Cleaners/Detergents	ACIDS/OXIDIZERS FLAMMABLES/COMBUSTIBLES	Battery Acid Paint Removers, De-rust Sprays Paints, Solvents	HEAT VIOLENT GAS GENERATION REACTION
CLEANING COMPOUNDS	Degreasers Carbon Removers Antifogging Compounds	DETERGENTS/SOAPS OXIDIZERS	Calcium Hypochlorite Sodium Nitrate Hydrogen Peroxide	HEAT FIRE HAZARD
COMPRESSED GASSES	Acetylene Helium Propane Ammonia Oxygen	HEAT SOURCES		FIRE HAZARD EXPLOSION HAZARD
CORROSIVE PREVENTIVE COMPOUNDS	Corrosive Inhibitors Chemical Conversion Compounds	ACIDS BASES, OXIDIZERS IGNITION SOURCES		FIRE HAZARD
DETERGENTS/ SOUPS	Detergents, Disinfectant, Scouring Powders, Sodium Hydroxide, Trisodium Phosphate, Potassium Hydroxide (Alalies/Bases/ Caustics)	ACID-CONTAINING COMPOUNDS	Battery Acid Paint Removers De-rust Sprays	VIOLENT REACTION HEAT
GREASES	Graphite Silicone Molydodenum	OXIDIZERS ALKALIES/BASES/ CAUSTICS		FIRE HAZARD
HYDRAULIC FLUIDS	Petroleum-Based Synthetic Fire-Resistant	CORROSIVES OXIDIZERS		HEAT VIOLENT REACTION
INSPECTION PENETRANTS	Petroleum-Based Dyes	CORROSIVES OXIDIZERS	Battery Acid Bleach Chrome, Hydrogen Peroxide, Paint Removers Ammonia	
LUBRICANTS OILS	Gen. Purpose Turbine, Gear, Vacuum, Weapon	CORROSIVES OXIDIZERS		EXPLOSION HAZARD
PAINTS	Primers, Enamels, Lacquers, Strippers, Varnish, Thinners	OXIDIZERS CORROSIVES		HEAT FIRE HAZARD
PHOTO CHEMICALS	Color and BW Bleaches/Stopbath Replenishers, Toners	ACIDS HEAVY METALS		HEAT FIRE HAZARD
POLISH/WAX COMPOUNDS	Buffing Compound Metal Polish Gen. Purpose Wax	CORROSIVES OXIDIZERS		HEAT, FIRE HAZARD VIOLENT REACTION

SOLVENTS (HYDROCARBONS)	Acetone, Methyl Ketone (MEK), Toluene, Xylene, Alcohols	CORROSIVES OXIDIZERS BATTERIES	Batter Acid Hydrogen Calcium Hypochlorite	HEAT FIRE HAZARD
THERMAL INSULATION	Asbestos Fiberous Glass Man-Made Vitreous	MATERIAL IS NOT REACTIVE KEEP DRY		NO REACTION
WATER THREATMENT CHEMICALS	Trisodium Phosphate Caustic Soda Citric/Nitric Acid	CORROSIVES OXIDIZERS HEAVY METALS		HEAT VIOLENT REACTION
OXIDIZERS	Chlorine Laundry Calcium Hypochlorite Calcium Oxide Hydrogen Lithium Hydroxide	PETROLEUM BASED MATERIALS FUELS, SOLVENTS, CORROSIVES, HEAT		FIRE HAZARD TOXIC GAS GENERATION
FUELS	Heating Oil Gasoline, Kerosene	CORROSIVES OXIDIZERS	Battery Acid Calcium Hypochlorite	FIRE HAZARD TOXIC GAS GENERATION
HEAVY METALS	Beryllium, Chromium, Lead, Magnesium, Nickel, Strontium, Tin, Zinc	CORROSIVES OXIDIZERS WATER TREATMENT/ PHOTO CHEMICALS		VIOLENT REACTION GENERATION OF TOXIC AND FLAMMABLE GAS
BATTERIES	Lead Acid Alkaine Lithium Hydroxide Dry Cell	SOLVENTS HEAVY METALS OXIDERS	Xylene, Toluene, Alcohol, Tin, Zinc, Chromium	HEAT VIOLENT REACTION TOXIC GAS GENERATION
PESTICIDES	Insecticides Fungicides Rodenticides Fumigants	CORROSIVES OXIDIZERS		TOXIC GAS GENERATION

BIO-CHEMICAL TERRORISM

BIO-CHEMICAL INFORMATION

AGENT	DESCRIPTION	AMOUNT	SYMPTONS	TREATMENT
Anthrax	A bacterium, with spore-forming rods, that lives in soil; infects humans by contact or inhalation of spores; produces an often fatal toxin.	One billionth of a gram.	Causes flu-like symptoms including high fever, cough and fatigue. Shock and death may occur within 24-36 hours.	Can be prevented with vaccine and treated with antibiotics —usually penicillin.
Botulinus	A bacterium that does not require oxygen (anaerobic bacterium) and causes a relatively slow onset of respiratory failure after exposure.	One billionth of a gram.	Dry throat, blurred vision and dizziness.	Can be prevented by using gas mask and protective clothing. Treated with an anti-toxin injection.
VX	A lethal chemical agent liquid that is odorless, colorless and vaporizes when it comes in contact with oxygen.	One drop or 10 milligrams.	Causes flu-like symptoms including high fever, cough and fatigue. Shock and death may occur within 24-36 hours.	Can be prevented by using gas mask and protective clothing.

BIO-CHEMICAL TERRORISM (con't)

BIO-CHEMICAL INFORMATION

Mustard Gas	A colorless and odorless liquid that turns brown in mixture and smells of garlic.		Watery eyes, burning lungs, itchy skin.	Can be prevented by using gas mask and protective clothing.
Sarin	A highly toxic agent that attacks the central nervous system.	100 milligrams	Causes severe headache, breathing difficulty, increased salivation.	Can be prevented by using gas mask and protective clothing.

BIO-CHEMICAL TERRORISM

A decision to "Shelter in Building" or evacuate must be made.

 **Principal's Office**

1.	Call 911 immediately for State Police and EMS.
2.	Contain possible bio-chemical contamination in plastic bin.
3.	Direct custodian to shut down heating, ventilation, air conditioning units and water supply throughout school.
4.	Activate procedures for Staff and Crisis team notification. Notify Superintendent of Schools or designee.
5.	Check air intake ducts—especially those lower than 20 feet above ground. NOTE: Air intake ducts with pre-filters do not provide protection from aerosolized bio-chemicals.
6.	If building is equipped with humidifiers, check water supply for evidence of contamination.
7.	Consult with Fire department officials as to whether to "Shelter in Building" or evacuate.
8.	Activate procedure for parent notification.
9.	Assist District and Local officials as needed.

Decision to Shelter: **Then:**

1.	Follow "Shelter in Place" procedure.

Decision to Evacuate: **Then:**

1.	Follow evacuation procedures.

BIO-CHEMICAL TERRORISM

SUSPICIOUS LETTERS or PACKAGES

 **Clerical/Office Staff**

 Principal's Office

1.	Do not shake or empty the contents of suspicious package.
2.	Place envelope or package in plastic container in designated area.
3.	Then leave room and close doors.
4.	Wash hands with soap and water.
5.	List all people who were in room. Give this list to both Local Health Authorities and Law Enforcement officials for follow-up investigations and advice.
6.	Call Postal Inspector to report receiving suspicious parcel.

1.	CALL 911 IMMEDIATELY TO REPORT THE INCIDENT OR THREAT.
2.	Contain possible biological contamination.
3.	Direct custodians to shut down heating, ventilation and air conditioning units.
4.	Activate procedures for Staff and Crisis Team notification. Notify Superintendent of Schools or designee.
5.	Request assistance and direction from emergency services and/or fire department officials on whether to "shelter in the building" or evacuate the building.
6.	Designate staff member or members to debrief anyone who may have seen a suspicious activity—especially near air intakes.
7.	Check air intake ducts—especially those lower than 20 feet above ground. NOTE: Air intake ducts with pre-filters do not provide protection from chemical attacks unless specified.
8.	If building is equipped with humidifiers, check water supply for evidence of biological contamination.
9.	Assist district and local officials as needed.

BIO-CHEMICAL TERRORISM (con't)

SUSPICIOUS LETTERS or PACKAGES

Checklist for Suspicious Letters/Packages

- ☒ Foreign Mail, Airmail or Special Delivery markings.

- ☒ Use of restrictive address, i.e., "Personal" or "Confidential."

- ☒ Excessive use of stamps instead of metered postage.

- ☒ Handwritten or poorly typed addresses.

- ☒ Incorrect titles.

- ☒ Use of titles instead of individual names.

- ☒ Misspellings of commonly used words.

- ☒ Oil stains or discolored envelope.

- ☒ No return address.

- ☒ Excessively heavy letter.

- ☒ Rigid envelope.

- ☒ Lopsided or uneven envelope.

- ☒ Protruding wires or metal foil.

- ☒ Excessive use of tape or paper.

- ☒ Visual distractions.

WATER SHORTAGE

 **Custodian**

1.	Assist officials in determining cause of shortage and in making repairs if that is the cause.
2.	If drought conditions, take precautions in bathrooms and other areas water is used.

 **Principal's Office**

1.	Notify building's occupants by PA announcement or messenger.
2.	Implement water conservation plan with School Sanitation. Arrange for bottled drinking water if shortage is prolonged.
3.	Notify Superintendent's office.
4.	File an incident report.

Teacher

1.	Continue normal educational duties, while reminding students to conserve water during regular school day.
2.	Eliminate activities which would unnecessarily waste water.

MEDICAL 3

Medical Problem or Injury
Bloodborne Pathogens
Head, Neck, or Back Injury
Fractures/Dislocations
Broken/Lost Teeth
Food Poisoning
Food Allergy/Reaction
Ingestion of Unknown Substance
Choking
Asthma Attack
Anaphylactic Shock/Bee Sting
Inhalants/Huffing
Bites—Animal, Human and Insect
Epileptic Seizures/Convulsions
Burns
Eye Injuries/Problems
Untimely Death

MEDICAL PROBLEM OR INJURY

Teacher/Adult on Scene

1.	Do not move child—keep stable and reassure them. Child could be moved if keeping them where they are appears dangerous (fire or explosion possibility) or inappropriate. If they were on playground in very cold weather, moving to warm place could be necessary. Cover with blanket if they can't be moved.
2.	Contact office and request 911 be called. If not near intercom or telephone, send a student to report to office.
3.	Report name of injured student and nature of problem or injury and request nurse.
4.	When appropriate, complete incident reports with nurse ASAP.
5.	Reassure other children who witnessed injury.

Principal's Office

1.	Call RN and be certain 911 has been called.
2.	Ensure parents or guardian is notified ASAP.
3.	Notify Superintendent.
4.	Complete incident report after speaking with witnesses and medical personnel.
5.	Notify Superintendent or designee.

 Principal's Office

1.	Upon notification, obtain student's emergency health information and go to site ASAP.
2.	Bring necessary medical supplies to site.
3.	Assess severity of injury or illness and, if appropriate, ensure 911 is called.
4.	Accompany child should it be necessary to transport them to a hospital by ambulance.
5.	Notify parent/guardian.

MEDICAL PROBLEM OR INJURY (con't)

A "serious" injury is defined as one in which there is no pulse, person is not breathing, or there is uncontrolled bleeding. Remember to provide only emergency care unless you receive instructions from medically trained person via radio or telephone.

If SERIOUS Problem: **Then:**

1.	Ensure 911 call for ambulance has been made.
2.	Stabilize student and immobilize injured parts if possible and administer first aid until medical personnel arrive.
3.	Check pulse in neck and if no pulse, begin CPR.
4.	Do not move unless location is dangerous (i.e., fire or fear of explosion).
5.	Ensure that Principal's Office is notified as soon as feasible.
6.	Have student's emergency health information available to accompany student to hospital.
7.	Obtain diagnosis; follow-up and file report.

A "minor" problem is usually best handled by taking a few moments to get the situation under control.

If MINOR Problem: **Then:**

1.	First adult on scene should remember to use common sense and remember ABC's of emergency assessment: - Make sure **A**irway is unobstructed - Be certain person is **B**reathing - Ensure **C**irculation of blood is maintained.
2.	Move student to Nurse's office for assessment.
3.	Administer first aid as necessary.
4.	Call student's physician if indicated on enrollment card; if appropriate, call parents.
5.	File incident report.

BLOODBORNE PATHOGENS

Anyone who could reasonably be expected to have contact with blood or potentially infectious bodily fluids while at work is covered by the OSHA standard. While not every school employee is likely to be exposed to bloodborne pathogens, each school employees should understand the dangers of infection and safe practices to minimize risk.

Teacher

1.	If victim is bleeding or if you could come in contact with saliva, semen, vaginal secretions, torn or loose skin or unfixed tissue or organs, **DO NOT TOUCH!**
2.	Ensure 911 is called for medical assistance if injury is severe.
3.	REDUCE RISK of exposure by using: Work practice controls Personal protective equipment Engineering controls Housekeeping Hepatitis B vaccine Playing it Safe by reacting not only with your heart but with your head!
4.	Be certain gloves and other protective equipment is used by personnel who could contact with blood, potentially infectious materials or mucous membranes or torn skin.
5.	Ensure vital signs are checked and assessment completed before allowing victim to be moved and defer all other actions to nurse, athletic trainer, physician or EMT.
6.	Use personal hygiene techniques to protect yourself from contamination by minimizing splashing, spraying, or spattering when attending to victim and by not eating, drinking, smoking, putting on cosmetics or handling contact lenses if there is likelihood of exposure.

Principal's Office

1.	Immediately call 911 and notify parent or guardian listed on emergency release form if injury is severe.
2.	Appoint staff member to obtain emergency health card from training room and take it to scene or hospital.
3.	Provide "First Responder Kits" in various locations to reduce threat of bloodborne pathogens. Kits should contain gloves, combination masks that protect eyes, nose and mouth, gauze and first aid equipment and a device for resuscitation.
4.	Assist with attending to victim and directing emergency personnel to site, assuring that Universal Precautions are taken.
5.	Be certain engineering controls i.e., physical or mechanical systems to eliminate hazards are available to anyone who is risking exposure.
6.	Remind those at scene of possibility of infection from contaminated sharp object i.e., Broken glass Sharp metal Needles Knives Exposed ends of wires on dental braces

BLOODBORNE PATHOGENS (con't)

 **Teacher**

7.	Remove Personal Protective Equipment (PPE) and gloves in proper manner and dispose of them promptly.
8.	Accompany injured student to hospital.
9.	Stay at hospital until relieved by parents or guardian.
10.	Act as liaison between hospital, Principal's office and athletic department.
11.	File report.
12.	Make follow-up visits and phone to check on victim's condition.

 **Principal's Office**

7.	Notify Superintendent or designee's office if athletic director has not done so.
8.	Ensure that good housekeeping procedures are used to clean and decontaminate all equipment and environmental working surfaces using appropriate disinfectant.
9.	Ensure good hand washing practices are used every time personnel remove gloves, if individual has come in direct contact with bodily fluids.

 **Custodian**

1.	If you are required to clean up blood or other bodily fluids be certain to: Wear appropriate PPE Use a solution of one part bleach to ten parts water Disinfect mops and cleaning tools after completing job.
2.	Report to supervision if any equipment needs to be replaced or disposed of after incident.

HEAD, NECK or BACK INJURIES

 Coach or Playground Staff

1.	Assess victim for symptoms of neck/ cervical spine or back injury, usually occurring during athletic activity.
2.	Immediately ensure 911 is called for medical assistance.
3.	Look for impaired level of consciousness, loss of movement or pain in neck/back.
4.	Leave in position found and immobilize by placing pillows or rolled blankets around entire body and cover to retain heat.
5.	Do not allow athlete to be moved except by medically trained personnel if serious injury is suspected and assume fractures.
6.	If complaining of neck pain, immediately **stabilize** player's head manually by holding the head. Be certain not to raise or lower chin or turn head.
7.	Assess consciousness, breathing, and pulse while waiting for emergency personnel.
8.	Ensure that first arriving medical person takes CSI precautions.
9.	Ensure vital signs are checked and assessment completed before allowing athlete to be moved.
10.	Defer all other action to athletic trainer, physician or EMT.
11.	Accompany injured athlete to hospital.
12.	Stay at hospital until relieved by parents or guardian.
13.	Act as liaison between hospital, Principal's office and athletic department.
14.	File report.
15.	Make follow-up visits and phone to check on athlete's condition.

 **Coach/Athletic Director**

1.	Immediately call 911 and notify parent or guardian listed on emergency release form.
2.	Appoint staff member to obtain emergency health card from training room and take it to scene or hospital.
3.	Notify Superintendent or designee's office.
4.	Assist with attending to victim and directing emergency personnel to site.

Principal's Office

1.	Notify parents if athletic director has not done so.
2.	Notify Superintendent or designee's office if athletic director has not done so.

 Teacher

1.	Notify nurse if injury occurs.
2.	Calm other students and comfort injured child.

FRACTURES/DISLOCATIONS

 **Teacher**

1.	If obvious distortion in shape of joint or if sound of bone snapping was audile, presume fracture.
2.	Call 911 immediately.
3.	Notify Nurse to assist with management of student.
4.	Immobilize affected area with pillows, rolled blankets and support injured area.
5.	After initial emergency, comfort other students.

 **Principal's Office**

1.	Ensure 911 is called.
2.	Notify nurse.
3.	Appoint a staff member to obtain emergency health information from enrollment cards.
4.	Assist Nurse with management of student.
5.	Ensure parents are notified ASAP.

 Nurse

1.	Determine severity of injury and ensure 911 has been called.
2.	Identify affected area and assume fracture if distortion in shape of joint or there is loss of movement to affected limb.
3.	Immobilize affected area with pillows or blankets and support injured area while waiting for assistance.
4.	Calm student while attending to problem by explaining what is going on in as calm a manner as possible.
5.	Accompany student to hospital if necessary.
6.	Contact parents and notify them of injury.
7.	Complete incident reports as soon as feasible.

BROKEN/LOST TOOTH

Teacher

1.	If tooth has been knocked out, rinse in clean water and wrap in wet cloth or plastic wrap and submerge in cold or ice water.
2.	Notify Nurse to assist with management of student.

Principal's Office

1.	Notify Nurse to assist with incident.
2.	Assist Nurse with management of student.

Nurse

1.	If tooth has been knocked out, ensure that it is rinsed in clean water and wrapped in wet cloth or plastic wrap and submerge in cold or ice water.
2.	Help student seek dental care immediately to facilitate successful re-implantation.
3.	If broken tooth, soak tip of cotton swab in oil of cloves and apply to tooth.
4.	Calm student while attending to problem by explaining what is going on in as calm a manner as possible.
5.	If problem caused by fall or facial injury, apply warm packs to side of face to lessen pain.
6.	Give aspirin or acetaminophen if allowed by parent emergency instructions.
7.	Contact parents and notify them of problem.

FOOD POISONING

Teacher

1.	Notify Nurse.
2.	Assist with those feeling affects of tainted food, until all students and staff are attended to.
3.	Assist with parent notification if necessary.
4.	Comfort other students even if not ill.

Nurse

1.	Determine severity of illness and how widespread.
2.	If severe problem, call 911 for ambulance; administer first aid until medics arrive.
3.	File appropriate reports with public health agencies.

IF NOT SEVERE PROBLEM:

1.	Administer first aid until parents arrive.
2.	Hand out to parents suggested treatment for mild food poisoning.
3.	File incident reports ASAP.

Principal's Office

1.	Call for Nurse.
2.	Appoint a staff member to pull appropriate emergency health information from enrollment cards.
3.	Notify cafeteria to take action.
4.	Notify parents to pick up ill students if medical personnel advise.
5.	Notify Superintendent/designee.
6.	Convene Crisis Team.
7.	Assist Nurse with management of ill students.
8.	Follow directions from public health agencies.
9.	Notify all parents as to occurrence.
10.	File appropriate reports with district and public health agencies.

Cafeteria Supervisor

1.	Close cafeteria.
2.	Secure items used in food preparation for examination and tests.
3.	Store samples of suspected menu items for examination.
4.	Remain available for examination by public health personnel.
5.	Follow any further directions from public health agencies.

FOOD or NUT ALLERGY/REACTION

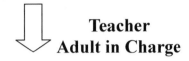

Teacher
Adult in Charge

1.	Notify Nurse and cafeteria staff that student with allergy has ingested allergic substance.

Nurse

1.	Determine severity of allergic reaction and what substance was inadvertently ingested.
2.	Call 911 for ambulance.
3.	Administer emergency allergic reaction medication if prescribed or first aid until medics arrive.
4.	File appropriate reports with public health agencies.
5.	File incident reports ASAP.

Principal's Office

1.	Call for Nurse and ensure 911 is called.
2.	Appoint a staff member to pull appropriate emergency health/allergy information from enrollment cards.
3.	Notify cafeteria to take action.
4.	Notify parents to pick up ill students if medical personnel advise.
5.	Notify Superintendent or designee.
6.	Convene Crisis Team.
7.	Assist Nurse with management of student.
8.	Follow directions from public health agencies.
9.	File appropriate reports with district and public health agencies.

Cafeteria
Supervisor

1.	Close cafeteria.
2.	Secure sample of items accidentally eaten for tests.
3.	Store samples of menu items for examination.
4.	Remain available for examinations by public health personnel.
5.	Follow any further directions from public health agencies.

INGESTION of UNKNOWN SUBSTANCE

 **Teacher**

 Nurse

	Teacher
1.	If student becomes ill or unstable, keep as stable as possible.
2.	Ensure 911 is called ASAP as time could be critical!
3.	If there is evidence i.e., pills, white powder, or any other unknown substance, **DO NOT TOUCH as some types of drugs can be absorbed through the skin!**
4.	Notify Nurse with name of ill student and confirm that 911 has been called.
5.	Notify Principal's office.
6.	Isolate witnesses and wait for State Police.
7.	Interview witnesses to determine if incident was a suicide attempt.
8.	Reassure other students.
9.	Complete incident reports ASAP.

	Nurse
1.	Call 911 ASAP, as time could be critical!
2.	Conduct an emergency assessment of victim's condition.
3.	If there is evidence i.e., pills, white powder, or any other unknown substance, **DO NOT TOUCH as some types of drugs can be absorbed through the skin!**
4.	If student is alert, ask for name of drug, how taken and at what time. Substance can be legal or illegal and student's health history should be checked ASAP!
5.	Administer first aid until ambulance arrives.
6.	Obtain emergency medical information from student file and give to emergency personnel.
7.	Document observations and findings including if evidence of a suicide attempt.
8.	Turn over any evidence to proper authorities.
9.	File incident report when feasible.

INGESTION of UNKNOWN SUBSTANCE (con't)

Principal's Office

1.	Facilitate 911 call if appropriate. Notify Police as per policy.
2.	Notify Superintendent or designee.
3.	Appoint an Administrator, Counselor, Social Worker or Nurse to contact a parent.
4.	State Police will contact parents and relay information regarding results of laboratory testing to determine identity of substance.
5.	Notify police as per policy.
6.	Convene school Crisis Team to determine postvention activities and how to transition from crisis management to aftermath in order to coordinate communication and needs in an organized way.
7.	Ensure proper communication and briefing of ALL appropriate personnel after incident.
8.	If a major incident both staff and students may need intensive counseling.

CHOKING

 Teacher
Adult in Scene

1.	If student is clutching throat and gasping followed by inability to cough, speak or breathe while eating, assume they are choking.
2.	In standing position, wrap arms around person from behind, make fist with one hand, covering it with the other.
3.	Place fist just above navel but under rib cage.
4.	Thrust fist sharply upward and back into person's abdomen.
5.	Repeat 4 times.
6.	If food is not dislodged, stand at the side and slightly behind victim.
7.	Place one hand on chest for support.
8.	Deliver 4 sharp blows with heel of other hand over spine and between shoulder blades.
9.	Repeat both maneuvers again until object has been dislodged.
10.	Sweep mouth with finger.
11.	Do not use this procedure if person is able to couth or make any noise. If person has been injured, do not move unless necessary.
12.	Ensure physician checks person as soon as possible.
13.	Reassure other children who observed incident.

 Principal's Office

1.	Call for Nurse and ensure 911 is called.
2.	Notify Nurse to assist and document incident.
3.	Notify parents if appropriate.
4.	Notify Superintendent or designee.

ASTHMA ATTACK

 **Teacher**

1.	If student is wheezing or having difficulty breathing/exhaling, and has history of asthma, presume they are having an asthma attack.
2.	Notify Nurse to assist with management of student.
3.	Check to see if student has asthma medication or inhaler available for immediate use.
4.	Keep child as calm as possible.
5.	Do not force asthmatic child to go outside in conditions, which could make attack worse.
6.	Reassure other children in class when incident occurred.

 **Principal's Office**

1.	Notify for Nurse and ensure 911 is called if appropriate.
2.	Appoint a staff member to pull emergency health information from enrollment cards.
3.	Assist Nurse with management of student.

 Nurse

1.	Determine severity of asthma attack. If severe, call 911 ASAP.
2.	Administer asthma medication if prescribed or first aid until medics arrive.
3.	Check for difficulty in exhaling, rapid heartbeat, pale, bluish skin, lips and nails.
4.	Calm student while attending to problem by explaining what is going on in as calm a manner as possible.
5.	If attack does not require 911, contact physician for further instructions, especially if attack does not subside within 30 minutes.
6.	Contact parents and notify them of attack.

ANAPHYLACTIC SHOCK from BEE STING

 Teacher

1.	Notify nurse that student with bee allergy has been stung.
2.	Get bee sting kit and administer antidote ASAP!
3.	Stay with student until Nurse or assistance arrives, keeping them as calm as possible.

 **Principal's Office**

1.	Ensure 911 is called immediately.
2.	Call for Nurse.
3.	Appoint a staff member to pull appropriate emergency health/allergy information from enrollment cards.
4.	Notify parents.
5.	Notify Superintendent or designee.

 **Nurse**

1.	Call 911 for ambulance.
2.	Administer emergency allergic reaction medication if necessary or first aid until medics arrive.
3.	Ensure parent or guardian is notified ASAP.
4.	File incident reports ASAP.

INHALANTS/HUFFING

Inhalant abuse is a form of drug abuse in which common products that can be sniffed to achieve euphoria are used to excess. These products include: glue, gasoline, magic markers, nail polish, room deodorizers, whip cream containers, cooking spray, turpentine, lighter fluid, typewriter correction fluid and refrigerant gases.

 **Teacher**

1.	Drunken appearance slurred speech, loss of coordination and bloodshot eyes without the smell of alcohol can be clues to use.
2.	Ensure 911 is called for medical assistance if impairment is severe.
3.	Check for chemical smell, rashes or sores around mouth or nose.
4.	Be certain gloves or other equipment is used by personnel who could contact with blood, vomit, potentially infectious materials or mucous membranes or torn skin.
5.	Accompany injured student to hospital.
6.	Remove Personal Protective Equipment (PPE) and gloves in proper manner and dispose of them promptly.
7.	Stay in hospital until relieved by parents or guardian.
8.	Act as liaison between hospital, Principal's office and parents.
9.	File Report.

Principal's Office

1.	If student is suspected of inhalant abuse, refer to school psychologist for treatment immediately.
2.	Notify parents immediately.
3.	Be alert to signs of inhalant use by students by including information in drug prevention curricula.
4.	Alert staff to report suspicious items i.e., soda cans containing something other than soda, plastic bags, rags and old socks that smell of chemicals.
5.	Consider monitoring students' access to abuseable substances in the school setting i.e., markers, glues, and paint products and typewriter correction fluid.
6.	Notify Superintendent or designee's if student is suspected of inhalant abuse.

Custodian

1.	If you are required to clean up blood or other bodily fluids be certain to: • Wear appropriate PPE • Use a solution of one part bleach to ten parts water • Disinfect mops and cleaning tools after completing job.
2.	Report to supervision if any equipment needs to be replaced or disposed of after incident.

ANIMAL, HUMAN or INSECT BITES

 **Teacher**

1.	Notify Nurse that student has been bitten.
2.	Wash wound thoroughly with soap and warm water and rinse well. If soap is not available, rinse bite thoroughly with warm water.
3.	Calm student by talking while attending to problem and explaining what you are doing.

 **Principal's Office**

1.	Notify for Nurse.
2.	Appoint a staff member to pull appropriate emergency health information from enrollment cards.
3.	If animal bite, try to trap animal if there is help available. Call dog or animal control officer for assistance.
4.	DO NOT take any action if there is a chance of getting bitten.
5.	If human bite, detain person who did the biting to determine how bite occurred.
6.	Notify public health authorities as required by law.
7.	Notify Superintendent or designee.

 **Nurse**

1.	Determine type of bite. If heavy bleeding, cover wound with thick, sterile gauze pad.
2.	If necessary call 911 for ambulance; administer emergency medical assistance until medics arrive.
3.	Do not try to close wound. If wound is deep, leave original gauze in place and add layers.
4.	Immobilize injured part with pillows or rolled blankets.
5.	Ensure parent or guardian is notified ASAP.
6.	File incident report when feasible.

EPILEPTIC SEIZURE or CONVULSION

 **Teacher**

1.	If student is involuntarily jerking muscles, unconscious, or loses control of bowel/bladder functions, presume they are having a seizure or convulsion, particularly if they have a medical history of this condition.
2.	Ensure 911 is called immediately.
3.	Have someone notify Nurse that you need assistance with management of student.
4.	Do not interfere with convulsive movements or give anything to eat or drink.
5.	Do not place anything between teeth. Place soft items or pillows around person if available and clear immediate area from harmful objects.
6.	Do not try to hold person down.
7.	Check to see if student medication is available for immediate use.
8.	Comfort other students.

 **Principal's Office**

1.	Ensure 911 is called immediately.
2.	Obtain emergency health information.
3.	Assist Nurse with management of student if necessary.
4.	Notify parents ASAP.

Nurse

1.	Determine severity of seizure or convulsion.
2.	Call 911 for ambulance; administer asthma medication if prescribed or first aid until medics arrive.
3.	If no medical history of epilepsy or convulsions, check for signs of chemical poisoning (burns on lips or mouth) or sudden abdominal or generalized pain.
4.	Calm student while attending to problem by explaining what is going on in as calm a manner as possible.
5.	When convulsion subsides, cool with wet lukewarm cloths on face and arms.
6.	Have student rest quietly and cover with blanket to retain body heat until emergency assistance arrives.

BURNS-Lighting, Electrical, Chemical, Sun

 **Teacher**

1.	If student is unconscious, check breathing.		1.	Call for Nurse and ensure 911 is called.
2.	In case of electrical shock, **DO NOT TOUCH PERSON or SOURCE.** Turn off mater switch or pull appliance plug.		2.	Appoint a staff member to pull emergency health information from enrollment cards.
3.	Notify Nurse to assist with management of student.		3.	Assist Nurse with management of student.

 **Principal's Office**

1.	Determine severity of burns and type of burn.
2.	If severe call 911 for ambulance. If necessary, administer first aid until medics arrive.
3.	If chemical burns, flush area thoroughly with water for at least five minutes to decontaminate.
4.	Gently move victim to safe, warm, sheltered area. Remove clothing and jewelry from burn area, cutting away if necessary. If clothing sticks to burn, **do not try to remove.**
5.	Calm student while attending to problem by explaining what is going on as calmly as possible.
6.	Contact parents and notify them of injury.

 TABLE TITLE

TYPES OF BURN	SYMPTOMS	TREATMENT
First Degree Burns	Redness of skin, pain, mild swelling. If over 10% of body, consider as third degree.	Apply cold, wet compresses or immerse in fresh, cold water-not ice or salt water-pain subsides.
Second Degree Burns	Deep reddening of skin, glossy appearance of skin from leaking fluid. Possible loss of some skin or blisters. If over 10% of body, consider as third degree.	Immerse in fresh, cold water-not ice or sale water-or apply cold compresses for 10-15 minutes. Gently dry with sterile gauze and cover with dry gauze. Do not damage blisters. If burns are extensive, seek immediate emergency treatment.
Third Degree Burns	Loss of all skin layers/painless, possible charring of skin edges involving more than a very small area.	Cover burn lightly with sterile gauze. Unless a chemical burn, do not use wet compresses or immerse in water. Obtain emergency assistance, checking breathing often. Elevate arms or legs if they are involved.

EYE INJURIES/FOREIGN MATTER

 **Teacher**

1.	Call for 911 assistance ASAP if a foreign object is penetrating eye.
2.	**DO NOT MOVE OBJECT** or try to remove it.
3.	Stabilize the object.
4.	Notify Nurse for assistance with management of student.

 **Principal's Office**

1.	Call for Nurse and ensure 911 is called.
2.	Appoint a staff member to pull emergency health information from enrollment cards.
3.	Assist Nurse with management of student.

 Nurse

1.	Determine severity of injury.
2.	If severe, call 911 for ambulance; administer first aid until medics arrive.
3.	If chemical burn of eye, turn head to one side and holding eyelids open, pour fresh water over eyes until assistance comes. Be certain to turn head to one side so affected eye is below to prevent residue from washing into unaffected eye.
4.	Calm student while attending to problem by explaining what is going on in as calm a manner as possible.
5.	Continue to rinse out eye or immobilize area until help arrives.
6.	Contact parents and notify them of attack.
7.	Complete incident report when feasible.

UNTIMELY DEATH

 **Teacher**

1.	Call 911, if person appears to have died. Notify Principal's office and the Nurse.
2.	Await 911 emergency personnel.
3.	Be certain not to disturb scene and turn control over to authorities upon arrival.
4.	Separate any witnesses if death occurred during the commission of a criminal act.
5.	If death has occurred due to unknown cause, it is still a crime scene that should be handled appropriately.
6.	Return students to classroom when advised and begin to identify students in need of treatment for shock.
7.	Complete incident reports ASAP.
8.	Continue to comfort and monitor students.

 **Principal's Office**

1.	Call 911 for police and ambulance.
2.	Convene school crisis team.
3.	Enable Police to take control of scene upon arrival.
4.	Notify Superintendent or designee's office.
5.	Inform staff and inform students.
6.	Facilitate investigations by civil authorities i.e., police, DCF.
7.	Announce counseling services and document students receiving counseling.
8.	Write notes to parents and express condolences.
9.	File an incident report.
10.	Follow up with counseling activities to assist personnel during period of grief.

 **Nurse**

1.	Provide privacy for victim.
2.	Document approximate time and specific observations.
3.	Provide copy of documented information to EMS for hospital personnel.

Early Dismissal Policy

Prior to Onset of Bad Weather

Tornado Safety Guidelines & Danger Signs

Conditions for Tornado Formation

Tornado Spotted in Area

After a Tornado

Hurricane Conditions

Hurricanes—Before

Hurricanes—During

Hurricanes—After

Earthquake Preparedness Measures

Earthquake Preparedness

During an Earthquake

After an Earthquake—First Hour Priorities

Flooding

EARLY DISMISSAL POLICY

Date

Dear Parents:

Please read with and discuss the emergency school closing, late opening or cancellation information with your children. Because of the possibility of Hurricane Bonnie or other major storms approaching the area, **please read this carefully and immediately**!

The following procedures will be followed in the event of cancellation or the delayed opening of schools due to **inclement weather** or other **emergency situations**. All decisions will be based on the most current weather forecasts available and observations of road conditions.

If the weather conditions indicate that schools will be closed, announcements will be made on the following radio and television stations by 6:30 a.m., whenever possible:

AM: _____   _____   _____
FM: _____   _____   _____
TV: _____   _____   _____

At times, the weather conditions may indicate the need to delay the start of school rather than close for the entire school day. In such cases, delayed opening announcement will be made on the above stations by 6:30 a.m.

In most cases of delayed opening, school will begin one hour later than usual. **Please note that all school transportation will be delayed the same amount of time as the school delay (i.e., one hour school delay = one hour bus delay).**

If it becomes necessary to delay the starting time by more than one hour, morning Pre-K and kindergarten classes will be canceled.

It is sometimes necessary to close schools earlier than usual because of emergency situations such as storms, loss of heart, etc. Parents should discuss this possibility with their children and make contingency plans for younger children to enter their home or go to a neighbor if no one is at home. In case of an early closing, the above stations will make announcements regarding times that students will be dismissed.

Please note that it is well advised to validate school cancellations or delays by tuning to a second station. If conflicting information is given, you may contact the bus coordinator's office by calling _____. Please do not utilize the bus coordinator's phone number unless you have attempted to validate the announcement and there is a problem.

Sincerely,

PRIOR or ONSET of BAD WEATHER

 **Teacher**

1.	Be aware of pre-designated WATCH and WARNING signals.
2.	WATCH—issued through PA announcement.
3.	WARNING—1 long bell of 5 seconds.
4.	Know shelter area your class is expected to reach.
5.	Be aware of any other specific assignments during TORNADO WATCH or WARNING.
6.	Move students to an inner hallway away from skylights or doors that might be blown open if necessary.
7.	Instruct students to sit on floor until "all clear" is given.
8.	Review "Drop & Tuck" procedure with class if appropriate.

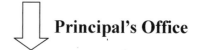 **Principal's Office**

1.	Review NOAA guidelines for safe and unsafe shelter areas.
2.	Designate tornado safe areas.
3.	Have a cell phone on hand with charged battery and ensure that appropriate personnel have that telephone number.
4.	Designate a special alarm system to indicate TORNADO WARNING if tornado is sighted and approaching.
5.	Use bullhorn or oral warning as backup alarm if electrical power fails.
6.	Ensure that staff and students are aware of differences between types of drills.
7.	Have regular tornado drills at least once per semester.
8.	Ensure staff and students are aware of differences between TORNADO WATCH and WARNING.
9.	Ensure staff and students are aware of tornado shelter areas.
10.	Instruct students how to "Drop and Tuck" if they hear a tornado warning signal.
11.	Have illustrations showing protective position posted on bulletin boards.
12.	Instruct students caught in outdoor open area how to take cover in nearest depression.
13.	Designate staff to monitor radio and TV warnings.
14.	Have battery-operated radio available.
15.	Assign specific duties to teachers and custodial staff.
16.	File incident reports ASAP if storm hits.

TORNADO SAFETY GUIDELINES
DANGER SIGNS

- **Severe Thunderstorms** with thunder, lightning, heavy rains and strong winds.
- **Hail** usually comes from dark-clouded skies as pellets of ice.
- **Roaring Noise** which sounds like a hundred trains or a crashing, thunderous sounds.
- **Funnel** with a dark, spinning "rope" or column stretching from the sky to ground or a sudden increase in wind.

- Remember that the National Weather Service issues a TORNADO WATCH when the possibility of tornadoes exists.
- A TORNADO WARNING is issued when a tornado is spotted or indicated on radar.
- Remember there may not be time for a TORNADO WARNING before a twister strikes. Tornadoes form suddenly. Teachers and students should know the difference between a WATCH and WARNING.
- Each school should be inspected and tornado shelter areas designated. Use interior hallways on the ground floor, which are NOT parallel to the tornado's path, which is usually from the southwest.
- Never use gymnasiums, auditoriums or other rooms with wide, free-span roofs.
- Avoid all windows and other glassed areas.
- Teachers and students should know their designated shelter areas.
- During a TORNADO WATCH, specific teachers or other staff members should be designated to monitor commercial radio or TV for TORNADO WARNINGS.

NOTE: The most dangerous locations in the building are usually along the south and west sides and at all corners.

- Weather spotters should keep an eye on the sky for dark, rolling clouds, hail, driving rain or a sudden increase in wind in addition to the telltale funnel or roaring noise. Precipitation or darkness often obscures tornadoes.
- Specific teachers should be assigned to round up students on playgrounds or other outdoor areas.
- When students are assembled in designated sheltered areas and if danger is imminent, instruct them to respond to a specific command, such as "Drop and Tuck."
- Students should assume a protective posture facing an interior wall.
- Remember most tornado deaths are caused by head injuries.

TORNADO SPOTTED/REPORTED in AREA

Bus Driver

1.	If tornado spotted, head away from path at a right angle.
2.	Try to find shelter under a bridge overpass.
3.	If sheltered under overpass, have students open window, then drop to floor and cover heads.
4.	Escort children in open area to low area such as a ditch, culvert or ravine.
5.	Account for all students.

Custodian(s)

1.	Shut off gas but not electricity.
2.	Ensure all exterior doors are closed to prevent wind tunnel effect.
3.	Hand out flashlights to teachers if time permits.
4.	Return to main shut-off for electricity.
5.	If tornado has hit shut off power if possible.
6.	Perform check of building following storm.

Teacher

1.	Evacuate students to pre-designated shelter area.
2.	Take roster.
3.	Take flashlight.
4.	Leave classroom door open.
5.	Have students sit on floor quietly, away from outside wall.
6.	Take roll and account for all students.
7.	Keep students calm and quiet.
8.	If in "Drop and Tuck," ensure students face wall in disaster position.
9.	If you sense tornado is imminent, give "Drop and Tuck" command.

Principal's Office

1.	Sound warning alarm immediately.
2.	Move occupants to shelter areas.
3.	Ensure appointed caretakers assist handicapped students.
4.	Issue "Drop and Tuck" over PA when judgment warrants.
5.	Account for all students.
6.	Shelter parents arriving at school but do not allow removal of students.
7.	Keep all exterior doors closed.
8.	Assist custodial staff in building assessment immediately after storm has passed and all persons are safe.

AFTER a TORNADO

 **Custodian(s)**

1.	Ensure gas and electricity have been shut off at main switches if building has been struck or damaged.
2.	Complete "Building Occupancy Checklist."
3.	Notify Administration as to damage assessment.
4.	Ensure any immediate safety issues are addressed

 **Teacher**

1.	Take roll ASAP.
2.	Report any injuries or missing students.
3.	Report by intercom or messenger but stay with students.
4.	Try to restore calm.
5.	Assist in first aid needed in your area.
6.	Await further instructions.

 **Principal's Office**

If Tornado Causes Injuries: **Then:**

1.	Contact custodian to ensure gas and electricity are turned off.
2.	Activate medical response by calling 911 for ambulances and fire department if necessary.
3.	Ensure all staff administers first aid until medical personnel arrive.
4.	Move injured as little as possible; all injured should be noted.
5.	Evacuate damaged area cautiously.
6.	Collect roll.
7.	Search for missing students or staff.
8.	Establish parent information response team ASAP.
9.	Assemble Crisis Team and deploy to specific assignment per plan.
10.	Ensure custodian checks for damage and file incident report.

If Tornado Passes Without Striking: **Then:**

1.	Be cautious, as there may be other funnels in area.
2.	Continue to monitor radio/TV for current advisory.
3.	Retain students in area until safe.
4.	Announce "all clear" to return to class.

HURRICANE CONDITIONS

Hurricane Conditions:

- Storm is less than 1,000 miles away.
- 24-36 hours from threat is a WATCH.
- Less than 24 hours from threat is a WARNING.
- Post-hurricane is immediately after storm ends.

	Hurricane Intensity Scale	
Category	Wind (mph)	Damage
1	74 to 95	Minimal
2	96 to 110	Moderate
3	111 to 130	Extensive
4	131 to 155	Extreme
5	155 and beyond	Catastrophic

HURRICANES - Before

Superintendent's Office

If Hurricane May Strike: **Then:**

1.	Track hurricane position and predicted path whenever storm enters Gulf of Mexico or threatens Atlantic Coast.
2.	Review hurricane shutdown plans and school closing with staff.
3.	Determine when to close school if appropriate.
4.	Connect—ED Activated

Teacher

Then:

1.	Assist in dismissal of students if deemed necessary.
2.	Store all books, papers and other equipment away from windows and above floor if possible.
3.	Move all audio-visual equipment to a secure, central location.
4.	Protect computers and other expensive equipment.

Nurse

Then:

1.	Ensure complete inventory of first aid supplies is available.
2.	Make inventory and location of first aid supplies known to appropriate staff.
3.	Review emergency pre-plan.

HURRICANES - During

 **Principal's Office**

During Hurricane Watch:

1.	Make preparation to close down school building when an official HURRICANE WATCH is issued.
2.	Ensure safe storage of all vital and expensive equipment.
3.	Advise transportation of special need students prior to school closing and dismissal of students.
4.	Dismiss students and close schools when directed by Superintendent or designee's office.
5.	Direct staff and other employees to close down their areas and leave school facility after students have left school.

If Hurricane Watch: Custodians

1.	Secure or move all portable and loose outside items to safe location inside.
2.	Secure all windows and glass.
3.	Start and test emergency generations to make certain they are operational.

If Hurricane Warning: Then:

1.	Turn off all boilers, gas and electrical devices except in areas designated as potential public shelters.
2.	Take any additional precautions considered necessary for protection of facility.
3.	If school is designated as a "public shelter," remain available to perform duties and responsibilities as a member of the Emergency Shelter Team.

HURRICANES - After

 **Principal's Office**

Immediately After Hurricane:

1.	With custodial staff, assess damage to building after storm has passed.
2.	With assistance from custodian use checklist assessment of Building's Operability.

Prepare List of Damage:

1.	Identify rooms that experienced such severe damage as to make them non-usable.
2.	Estimate earliest date for classes to resume if repair work is required.
3.	Submit damage form to Superintendent.
4.	Assist maintenance staff and safety officials to physically assess repairs needed.
5.	Determine schedule for school to reopen.
6.	File incident report.

Immediately After Hurricane:  Teachers

1.	Assist Principal on all duties that may be assigned to get school back into educational process.

Immediately After Hurricane:  Nurse

1.	Assist Principal on all duties that may be assigned to get school back into educational process.

Immediately After Hurricane:  Custodians

1.	Accompany Principal to assist in damage assessment.
2.	Assist Principal in filling out checklist for assessment of building's operability.
3.	Assist maintenance and safety officials in scheduling and overseeing repair work.
4.	Determine schedule of work to be done.

EARTHQUAKE PREPAREDNESS MEASURES

Potential Hazards:

- **Windows**: Non-tempered glass will shatter and gouge whatever it hits.
- **Lighting Fixtures: Fixtures** may fall and break; fluorescent bulbs will fall and break.
- **Ceilings**: Improperly installed ceilings may come down. Glued tiles may fall. Ducts may fall.
- **Chemical Spills**: In chemistry labs, cafeterias and custodial supply closets, chemical bottles can fall and break creating toxic fumes, combustible mixtures, exposed corrosives.
- **Furnishings and Miscellaneous Items**: File cabinets may fall over or fly across the room. Freestanding bookcases, lockers, shelves and contents will fall over. Heavy objects such as TV's, typewriters and computers may fly through the air. Screens and maps may become projectiles. Pianos will roll.
- **Compressed Gas Cylinders, Gas Appliances and Water Heaters**: All of these may pull away from the wall, become projectiles and create other gas hazards.
- **Gas Lines**: Lines will rupture. If gas lines are near a sparking wire or arcing motor, an explosion could result.
- **Basements and Electrical Supply**: Water pipes may rupture. Basements may flood deeply. Electrical switching mechanisms may become inaccessible.
- **Wall-Mounted and Hanging Objects**: Clocks, maps, fire extinguishers, hanging plants will all pull free and become projectiles.

Protective Measures

- **Install transparent, shatter-resistant** security film on windows. Install tempered glass in door panels.
- **Support fixtures and bulbs** with chains or strapping attached to studs and heavy metal structures.
- **Support ducts with strapping** attached to studs and heavy metal structures.
- **Install removable retraining bars** across the front of shelves. Post warning signs in areas of hazardous chemicals. Use careful labeling and segregate potentially dangerous reactionary mixtures.
- **Multiple rows of shelves** or lockers can be secured to overhead channel-shaped (not flat) metal bars attached to studs. Secure single shelves with heavy right-angle brackets and 2" or larger molly bolts to a wall stud or floor anchor. Keep file drawers latched when not in use. Move most heave objects to lower levels. When possible, secure with brackets and bolts.
- **Secure gas appliances and tanks** to wall studs with 2 metal or nylon belts; one should be about 1" above the floor.
- **Install automatic gas shut-off valves** to main intake line. Train custodians, cafeteria workers and lab students to shut off all gas lines before dropping to the floor.
- **Eliminate these items** when possible or secure with brackets, bolts and metal straps to wall studs.

> Although an earthquake may not occur during the childhood of your students, earthquake safety lessons learned at school will stay with them. If budgetary priorities limit scope of earthquake safety program, i.e., retrofitting your facility, you will make a difference if the most you do is conduct earthquake drills!

EARTHQUAKE PREPAREDNESS

 **Principal's Office**

1.	Recognize potential hazards and implement protective measurers.
2.	Train staff and students about earthquakes and have drills to practice emergency procedures.
3.	Determine who is trained in various rescue measures and assign responsibility.
4.	Predetermine emergency evacuation signal if PA is inoperable.
5.	Be aware school may be isolated from rescue officials and that staff may need to be self-sufficient.
6.	Prepare procedures for releasing students after earthquake.
7.	Establish emergency release area.
8.	Ensure emergency medical forms are movable and taken to site.
9.	Do not permit students to walk home.
10.	Advise parents of this special release procedure.
11.	Contact American Red Cross for information, which could be helpful.

DURING AN EARTHQUAKE

Whether indoors or outdoors, take action at first indication of ground shaking.

If Indoors in a Room: **All Staff and Students**

1.	Stay inside.
2.	Move away from windows, shelves and heavy objects or furniture that may fall.
3.	Take cover under a table or desk, not in a doorway.
4.	"Drop and Tuck."
5.	If the table or desk moves, hold the legs and move with it.

If Indoors in Hall, Stairway Or Open Area:

Then

1.	Move to the interior wall.
2.	Turn away from windows.
3.	"Drop and Tuck."

If Indoors in Lab, Kitchen, Or Boiler Room:

Then

1.	Extinguish all burners.
2.	Stay clear of hazardous chemicals that may spill.
3.	Take cover under a table or desk and move with it.

If Outdoors:

Then

1.	Move to an open space away from buildings and overhead power lines.
2.	Lie down or crouch.
3.	Keep looking around for potential hazards which may force you to move.

If On a School Bus:

Then

1.	Stop bus away from power line, bridges, overpasses and buildings.
2.	Students should remain in seats and hold on.

AFTER an EARTHQUAKE

First Hour Priorities

 **Custodian and Cafeteria Staff**

1.	SHUT OFF all gas and electricity at main switches.
2.	SHUT OFF all gas appliances and motors.
3.	Assist with first aid of injured.
4.	When appropriate, check facilities for damage.
5.	Complete "Building Operability Checklist."

 Nurse

1.	Administer first aid by triage.
2.	Attend to those most seriously injured.

Teacher

1.	Stay under shelter until shaking stops.
2.	If classroom is in imminent danger of fire, evacuate class immediately.
3.	Review evacuation routes with students if not in imminent danger.
4.	Check students for injuries and report critical injuries to office, accounting for all students.
5.	Administer critical first aid yourself, as help may be a long time in coming.

Principal's Office

1.	Perform First Hour Priorities.
2.	Stay under shelter until shaking stops.
3.	Make quick assessment and decide whether to evacuate; call 911.
4.	Signal evacuation with whatever means available.
5.	Alert staff to known hazards along route or blocked exits.
6.	Follow evacuation procedures.
7.	Keep this book and cell phone with you.
8.	Be prepared to respond quickly to injuries, fires, hazardous materials and trauma.
9.	Remember all may need to be self-sufficient for hours or days.
10.	File incident report.

AFTER an EARTHQUAKE (con't)

First Hour Priorities

 **Teacher**

If Told to Evacuate: **Then**

1.	Decide whether students in your area can be moved.
2.	Stay with critically injured students.
3.	Make arrangements to evacuate others.

If Evacuating: **Then**

1.	Be alert for hazards and be prepared to "Drop and Tuck."
2.	Account for all students again.
3.	Calm and reassure frightened students.
4.	Release students only to appropriate adults with help of Red Cross or police; keep record of releases.

FLOODS/HIGH WATER

**Preparedness Before
School Opens:**   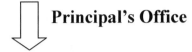 **Principal's Office**

1.	During heavy rains, consult with Superintendent or designee as to whether or not to open the school.
2.	Assess if any water problems in facility.

If School Is Open: **Then**

1.	Assign staff member to monitor TV and radio weather advisories.
2.	Assign staff member to keep eye on entry roads for inaccessibility.

If School Must Evacuate: **Then**

1.	Consult with Superintendent or designee to arrange for early dismissal and transportation of students.
2.	Activate procedure for parent notification.
3.	Ensure students are safe and that transportation/ evacuation is complete.
4.	Protect contents of building by moving books, files and other items from floors and bottom shelves.

FLOODS/HIGH WATER (con't)

Bus Drivers

1.	In advance, locate high ground areas along regular route.
2.	Watch for flooding in highway dips, low areas and bridges.
3.	DO NOT ATTEMPT to drive through dips of unknown depth.
4.	Be especially cautious at night when it is harder to recognize dangers.
5.	If part of route is impassable, radio manager for route suggestions.

If Vehicle Stalls:

Then

1.	In mildly flowing water which is not above the children's knees, abandon bus to higher ground keeping in mind FLASH FLOOD MAY BE IMMINENT.
2.	In deep or fast flowing water, act quickly to save students and others. Ask passersby for help as YOU MAY HAVE ONLY SECONDS!

Transportation Office

Preparedness Before School Opens:

Then

1.	Listen to local radio and TV for flash flood warnings or flooding in specific areas.
2.	Send emissaries to areas known to be flood prone to assess their accessibility.
3.	Determine whether roads are presently passable.
4.	Determine whether roads are likely to be passable when school opens.
5.	Evaluate whether roads are likely to flood during school day.
6.	Advise Superintendent or designee of assessment.

If School is Open:

Then

1.	Be prepared to reroute buses to more passable roads.
2.	Continue to monitor weather advisories during the day.
3.	Inform Superintendent of changes in assessment that may require early dismissal.

STUDENT WELFARE 5

Reported Missing or Runaway Student
Unauthorized Removal of Student
Suspected Child Abuse
Hearing of Potential Walkout
Pre-Plan for Student Walkout
During a Student Walkout
After Walkout

MISSING or RUNAWAY STUDENT

During School Hours - after student has been listed as "Present" or if student doesn't report for school after taking bus.

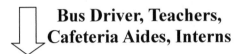

Bus Driver, Teachers, Cafeteria Aides, Interns

1.	Report to Principal immediately if you have reason to believe a student is missing at any time during school hours.
2.	Search campus, including an "all call" on PA.

Principal's Office

1.	Obtain registration form and photo from files.
2.	Search campus, including an "all call" on PA.
3.	Call parent or those listed on emergency release form.
4.	Advise parents that you are calling police.
5.	As soon as student is missing, initiate investigation to rule out foul play and to assist in locating child.
6.	If parents are unavailable, call police and keep trying to reach parents.
7.	Notify Superintendent or designee's office.
8.	Do not release any information to media; refer media inquiries to Superintendent's office.
9.	When police arrive at school, work closely with them.
10.	If student is located, notify parents immediately.

MISSING or RUNAWAY STUDENT (con't)

After School Hours - when student is missing between home and school.

 **Principal's Office**

1.	Begin proper procedures when parent or caregiver has called school to advise of missing student.
2.	Search campus including "all call" on PA.
3.	If student is bus rider, call Transportation Office and have them check with bus driver to determine if student used regular bus route.
4.	Advise parent or caregiver to contact alternate caregivers and friends.
5.	Advise caller or parent you will be calling police IMMEDIATELY.
6.	Ask caller to call again if student is located.
7.	Obtain missing student's registration form and photo from files to give to police.
8.	Check with children at student's bus stop.
9.	If student is a young child who is possibly lost, staff should drive child's usual route to school.
10.	Determine if there is a custody or other type of issue within the family.
11.	Notify Superintendent or designee's office and refer media questions to Superintendent's office.
12.	When police arrive at school, work closely with them. They will take control of situation.
13.	If student is located, notify parent immediately.
14.	File incident report.

UNAUTHORIZED REMOVAL of STUDENT

 **School Secretary**

1.	Use preventative actions and clearly communicate with proper school personnel if there is a custody issue with certain children/families.
2.	Have list of students on desk who are not to be release to anyone except a specific person or other special instructions.
3.	Red flag enrollment cards and emergency cards of such students.
4.	Check with custodial parent or guardian for approval before releasing child to anyone else. Ensure bus drivers are informed as to issues.
5.	Record time and date of telephone approval.
6.	Verify identity of parent with return call to parent's telephone number listed in student's folder.
7.	Record on student's enrollment card changes in custody after seeing court document.
8.	Keep copy of that document on file.
9.	Keep any student who seems reluctant to go with pick-up person.
10.	Ask for person's driver license number and record name and number.
11.	Notify custodial parent or guardian of student's reluctance; abide by parent's wishes.
12.	Ensure that coaches, custodians, playground supervisors, day care staff are all aware of circumstances surrounding particular children to avoid errors, especially at end of school day.
13.	In event of unauthorized removal **NOTIFY PRINCIPAL IMMEDIATELY!**

Teacher

1.	Report to Principal's office if an unauthorized person has removed a child.
2.	Assist secretary with above activities if requested.

Principal's Office

1.	Use good judgment; secretary calls police and guardian.
2.	Get license plate number if car involved.
3.	Call 911.
4.	Notify parent or guardian listed on student's emergency card.
5.	Notify Superintendent or designee's office.
6.	Do not release any information to media; refer inquiries to Superintendent's office.
7.	When police arrive, work closely with them.
8.	File incident report when feasible.

SUSPECTED CHILD ABUSE

 **Teacher**

1.	Report any suspected abuse or neglect of students with all relevant physical or mental information to Principal.
2.	Remember that each person to whom the child discloses abuse or neglect has responsibility to respond and report orally to children's protective services. In Connecticut: **(DCF) Hot Line 1-800-842-2288**
3.	File incident report.

Nurse

1.	Observe student and make assessment of suspected abuse or neglect.
2.	Ensure proper reporting procedures are followed.

If Abuse or Neglect is Determined or Suspected: **Then**

1.	Notify Principal and State Police.
2,	Follow DCF Guidelines.

HEARING of PLANNED STUDENT WALKOUT

Upon hearing of potential Walkout, **contact Police immediately!**

 **Teacher**

1.	Report to Principal's office.

 **Principal's Office**

1.	Identify issues and/or concerns that have led up to potential walkout.
2.	Obtain date, time and names of students involved.
3.	Determine course of action to avert walkout.
4.	Notify Superintendent's office.
5.	Call Police as appropriate.
6.	Meet with faculty to inform them of potential walkout.
7.	Meet with student leaders and student council to explain situation. Clear up rumors and avert walkout.
8.	Meet with community leaders to enlist support to avert walkout.

PRE-PLAN for STUDENT WALKOUT

 Principal's Office

1.	Coordinate with Police and assign staff to "supervision schedule."
2.	Pre-plan to have teachers at specific locations in halls or on grounds to supervise (i.e., fire alarms).
3.	Instruct teachers to take attendance before and after time of walkout.
4.	Instruct teachers to prepare absentee list to document names of students to walkout.
5.	Instruct teachers to watch actions and comments so as not to aggravate walkout situation.
6.	Designate person to videotape students and/or adults who participate, if appropriate.
7.	Emphasize to person making videotape the importance of a record for identification purposes and documenting verbal communications.
8.	Confer with Superintendent or designee for advice and decision-making.
9.	If a serious situation has occurred and State Police have taken over scene, media information will be given by Public Information Officer who handles media in serious and high profile cases.
10.	Ensure that no leaks to the media occur which could jeopardize investigation.

DURING a STUDENT WALKOUT

 **Teacher**

1.	Report to Principal's Office.

 **Principal's Office**

1.	Instruct staff to allow students to leave.
2.	Do not stop students from leaving.
3.	Ensure videotape is filming students, outsiders or adults participating, if appropriate.
4.	Announce on the intercom system "We want you to go to class."
5.	Wait 5 minutes to give students initial opportunity to return to class.
6.	Instruct hall duty personnel to conduct "hall sweep" to clear halls of students after 5 minutes.
7.	Ensure all students are either in class or outside.
8.	Ring bell or use bullhorn to encourage students to return.
9.	Monitor ongoing situation.
10.	Communicate current status of walkout to Superintendent or designee.

AFTER a STUDENT WALKOUT

 **Principal's Office**

1.	Instruct teacher to take attendance each period to determine students who participated in walkout.
2.	Be responsible for developing list of all students who walked out.
3.	Contact parents or guardians of walkout students to arrange for return of each student the next day.
4.	Inform parents or guardians of disciplinary action.
5.	Develop a system for admitting students back to school.
6.	File incident report.

MEDIA RELATIONS 6

Interaction with Media

INTERACTION with MEDIA

 ## Superintendent/Principal's Office

1.	All media contact will be deferred to Superintendent, Principal or Media Liaison designee.
2.	Staff should take measures to limit media access on school grounds to designated areas.
3.	Do not allow media access to students either on school buses or school grounds.
4.	Schedule press conference once crisis has passed. Stick to facts and give reasons for inability to comment. Control message and focus on well being of students.
5.	Know state laws and Board of Education policies concerning release of names.
6.	Remember priorities are to provide accurate information and to assure student well being and confidentiality.

MEDIA LIAISON RESPONSIBILITIES

 Principal or Media Liaison

1.	Prior to an incident, when the building Media Liaison is identified, plan a way of having all media contact funneled through Media Liaison designee.
2.	Media Liaison should clarify and become familiar with building and district policies concerning media.
3.	Investigate ways to contain media and discuss if they would be allowed on school grounds or to a pre-determined media designated area.
4.	Act as liaison between police Public Information office.
5.	Decide whether to limit media access on school grounds to designated areas.
6.	Decide under what circumstances media would be allowed to talk with individual students.
7.	Work with Superintendent on pre-planning of press conference locations and content once a crisis passed. Focus on well being of students.
8.	Familiarize yourself with state laws and board policies concerning release of names and handling of media.
9.	Remember priorities are to provide accurate information and to assure student well being and confidentiality.

MEDIA LIAISON DURING A CRISIS

 Principal or Media Liaison

1.	Identify building Media Liaison to media and, have al media contact funneled through Media Liaison designee.
2.	Identify persons available for interviews and announce location and time if possible, making certain individual has time to anticipate questions and formulate answers.
3.	Announce whether media will be allowed on school grounds or to a pre-determined media designated area.
4.	Act as liaison between State and local police Public Information spokesman if one is assigned to crisis.
5.	Try to ascertain questions prior to press conference if possible.
6.	Work with Superintendent to arrange press conference, announce location.
7.	Focus on providing honest, clear, direct interview and press conference.
8.	Work within state laws and board policies concerning release of names. Focus on well being of students.
9.	Priority is to provide accurate information and to assure student well being and confidentiality.
10.	Following crisis, schedule follow-up meeting with faculty and students who were interviewed by media.
11.	Have follow-up meeting with media, public information personnel if necessary.

CRISIS TEAM 7

Overview of Crisis Response Plan
Goals
Awareness and Education
Mission Statement
Team Members and Roles
Crisis Team Calling Tree
Staff Notification

OVERVIEW of CRISIS RESPONSE PLAN

The _____ School Crisis Team has prepared a Crisis Response Plan, which attempts to describe actions, roles and responsibilities to be taken by staff in response to:

- Violence
- Criminal Activity
- Medical or other Emergency Health situations
- Natural disasters
- Sudden death
- Suicide
- Child Abuse
- Substance Abuse

GOALS

The Crisis Response Plan is being established to:

- **Plan** ahead for incidents to students and staff
- **Reduce** risk of physical harm
- **Stabilize** any situations which may arise
- **Assure** effective decision making by planning proactively
- **Communicate** accurate information during times of crisis
- **Provide** psychological first aid and support
- **Re-establish** control
- **Return** to normal
- **Assure** follow up during postvention period

AWARENESS and PROFESSIONAL DEVELOPMENT

In order to have an effective Crisis & Emergency Response Plan, members of the _____ School community must know about this plan.

Activities, which should occur, include:

- Professional Development and training for all school staff
- General awareness for student body (i.e., crisis procedures, resources for help)
- Parent awareness of Plan's existence
- Specialized training for administrators and pupil support staff
- Providing local Emergency Management with this manual and any updates

MISSION STATEMENT

_____ SCHOOL
Crisis Team's Mission

TO:

- Provide the _____ **School** community with a Crisis and Emergency Management response plan for potential situations of physical danger and/or emotional trauma.
- Educate the members of the community of the Crisis and Emergency Management response plan's existence and content.
- Coordinate implementation of the plan during times of crisis and emergencies.

CRISIS TEAM MEMBERS and ROLES

_____   Chair

_____   Vice Chair

_____   Coordinator(s), Counseling Services

_____   Principal, Ex Officio

_____   Staff Notification Coordinator

_____   Communication Coordinators

_____   Crowd Manager

_____   Emergency Action Plan

_____   Parent(s)/Community Liaison

CRISIS TEAM CALLING TREE

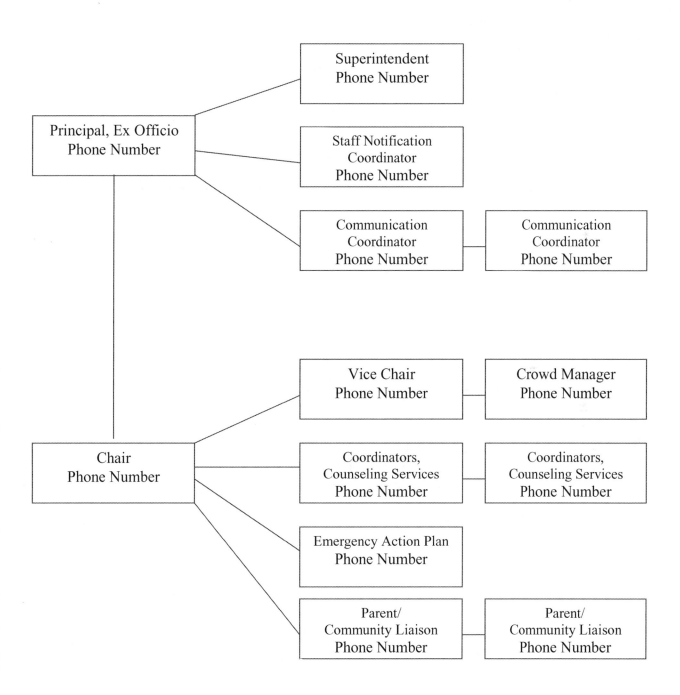

STAFF NOTIFICATION

When Crisis Occurs Outside School Day: Prior to Next School Day:

1.	Staff will be called via phone tree and given initial crisis information and staff meeting time.
2.	At meeting, staff will receive: • More detailed information about the crisis • Modifications to usual traffic flow/crowd management of building • Suggestions for class discussion, if needed, or response to students concerning incident • Information on availability and location of counseling for students and staff • Guidelines for dissemination of information to parents, media, and public • Explanation of resources available to help teachers and staff deal with the crisis • Time of follow-up meeting to evaluate response plan and plan continued response

When Crisis Occurs During School Day: Then:

1.	Follow the appropriate procedures per Crisis & Emergency Management manual.
2.	Following the "all clear," Crisis Team will meet and formulate a Crisis Response Plan.
3.	Ensure classroom contact personnel go to classrooms ASAP to inform staff as to what has happened and what has been planned.
4.	Announce time for a general staff meeting following student dismissal to asses student/staff need and plan further crisis response.

CRISIS TEAM PROCEDURES

CRISIS DURING SCHOOL DAY

When Crisis Occurs During
School Day: Then:

1.	Crisis Team members will follow Emergency Action Plan Procedures as per plan.
2.	Following the "all clear," Principal will contact Chair and Vice Chair to inform them of known facts and establish team meeting time.
3.	Chair and Vice Chair will inform remainder of team about time and date of meeting. Need for full staff meeting will be established.
4.	Crisis Team will meet ASAP.
5.	Principal will inform team of all facts.
6.	Team will discuss and determine appropriate level of involvement.
7.	Team will determine components of response plan including: • Support to students/families involved • Staff notification • Crowd management • Media Coordination • Involvement of community services • Level of parent involvement • Necessary coverage for team members to carry out crisis response duties
8.	Classroom contact personnel will be confirmed.
9.	Agenda and/or plan for staff meeting will be established.
10.	Set time for progress update meeting.
11.	Establish time for general staff meeting following student dismissal.
12.	Team members will perform crisis response duties.
13.	Hold a follow-up meeting to evaluate response plan and identify strengths and weaknesses.

CRISIS OUTSIDE SCHOOL DAY

When Crisis Occurs Outside School Day: **Then:**

1.	Notify Principal of the crisis.
2.	Principal will contact Chair and Vice Chair to inform them of known facts and establish team meeting time.
3.	Chair and Vice Chair will inform remainder of team about time and date of meeting. Need for full staff meeting will be established.
4.	Phone tree will disseminate initial crisis information and staff meeting time if need established.
5.	Principal will inform team of all facts at meeting.
6.	Team will discuss and determine appropriate level of involvement.
7.	Team will determine components of response plan including: • Support to students/families involved • Staff notification • Student notification • Crowd management • Media Coordination • Involvement of community services • Level of parent involvement • Necessary coverage for team members to carry out crisis response duties
8.	Agenda and/or plan for staff meeting will be established (determined by individual school).
9.	Set time for progress update meeting.
10.	Establish time for general staff meeting following student dismissal.
11.	Team members will perform crisis response duties.
12.	Team members will attend progress/update meeting.
13.	Hold a follow-up meeting to evaluate response plan and identify strengths and weaknesses.

ALARM SYSTEM and SIGNALS

When Crisis Occurs on School Grounds:

FIRE EMERGENCY: Then:

1.	Alarm sounds.
2.	911 will be notified and emergency personnel will control scene upon arrival.
3.	Building is evacuated according to fire drill guidelines posted inside each classroom door.
4.	Custodians only may use fire extinguishers at their discretion.

CLASSROOM or SCHOOL BOMB or TERRORIST THREAT: Then:

1.	Notify main office of threat and who is making it, if possible or if known.
2.	Call 911 immediately.
3.	Notify Administrative Team of crisis to make a decision after evaluation of situation.
4.	IF EVACUATION IS NECESSARY, instructions will be relayed to classrooms, i.e., opening windows and evacuation route to follow.

COMBATIVE CHILD or CHILD IN CRISIS: Then:

1.	Announcement made over intercom for all students to stay in classrooms until further notice.
2.	Next action would be dependent upon age of child. Children in Grade 4 and under should be able to be controlled by staff.
3.	If not in control or over Grade 4 student involved, notify 911.
4.	When situation is under control, announce "All Clear" over the intercom.

ALARM SYSTEM and SIGNALS (con't)

SEVERE WEATHER
WARNING: Then:

1.	If a severe weather alert is issued, teachers will be instructed over intercom to move students to an inner hallway, away from skylights or doors that might be blown open.
2.	Students should sit on the floor until "All Clear" is given.

CRISIS TEAM
RESPONSIBILITIES: Then:

1.	Administrative Team should be notified when any situation that is defined as a crisis occurs. Crisis Team should be briefed as to nature of crisis.
2.	Crisis Team assesses crisis and relays information to main office, as necessary.
3.	Code words will be used between assessment team and main office staff before an "All Clear" is given.

SET UP of EMERGENCY COMMAND CENTER

General Overview

An Emergency Operations Center will be set up when one or more outside agencies are summoned.

Knowing who is in charge legally at a scene of mass confusion can be crucial.

Generally, the following rules apply:

INCIDENT TYPE	PERSON IN CHARGE
Motor Vehicle Accidents	Fire Chief or designee
Hazardous materials and/or Dangerous Substances	Fire Chief or designee
Medical/Injuries to Individuals	Fire Chief or designee
Criminal Scene	State or Local Police

ZERO TOLERANCE POLICY/Example Procedures

Zero Tolerance

"Zero Tolerance" is a term which over the last several years has been used more and more by individuals in government, at schools, and in the news media to describe the degree to which we, as a society, should be willing to accept (or tolerate) certain kinds of behavior. For example, to what degree should we be willing to accept the use of drugs or the possession of weapons by students on campus? And to what degree should we be willing to accept the consumption of alcohol by teenage drivers or minors at school? Many of those who have used the term "zero tolerance" have argued that our society's degree of acceptance should be zero (or not at all). In some cases, legislative bodies and/or school officials have passed laws or developed policies based on notions of zero tolerance. In most cases, this has been done as a way to crack down on behaviors that society or schools are simply no longer willing to accept. Others have argued, however, that many zero tolerance policies or programs are simply unrealistic, arbitrary, and often unfair. For example, students have recently been expelled from schools under zero tolerance programs designed to prohibit the possession or use of weapons or alcohol at schools or for possessing a Swiss Army knife or having alcohol in their hotel rooms while on a school-sponsored field trip. Whether fair or not, parents and kids should realize that in a world where many believe that kids abuse the law, such policies are becoming more common. As a result, schools, as well as the courts, are finding it more difficult to accept any excuse for conduct that they believe is simply no longer acceptable. Try to become aware of such programs or policies in your community.

Safe Schools and Violence Prevention Office

The California Legislature enacted laws labeled "zero tolerance" that called for a mandatory recommendation for expulsion from school for those students who committed any of the following acts, unless the punishment was considered inappropriate for the circumstance of the act:

- causing serious physical injury to another person, except in self-defense;
- possessing any knife, explosive, or other dangerous object of no reasonable use to the student on campus or at school-related events;
- unlawfully possessing or selling a controlled substance, except for the first offense of less than one ounce of marijuana; and
- robbing or extorting another person.

School districts that have instituted "zero tolerance" policies have reported success by taking a strong stand on school violence. For example, San Diego Juvenile Court Judge William Pate reports that when the city schools implemented and formalized their zero tolerance policy on violence, crimes against persons and property on school campuses decreased by 343 incidents. Although the reported data covered only the last quarter of the school year, the Judge considered the 15 percent reduction significant.

Youth expelled from school cannot enroll in another school in the district nor in another district during the period of expulsion (one full calendar year for possession of a firearm on campus), unless it is a district community day school (*Education Code* Sections 48660-48666, effective July 1, 1996) or a county community school (*Education Code* Section 48915.2). Until districts initiated community day schools in 1996-97, expelled students only had county community schools as an educational option. Most county community schools do **not** accept youth in elementary schools and often do not accept students from middle or junior high school. Thus, those youth not enrolled in an alternative educational setting are in the community during school hours, often without supervision. The educational and social setbacks from expulsion are often associated with higher dropout rates and daytime criminal activity committed by youth. Educational placements for these youth are critical for their advancement academically and for the well being of the community.